Student-Engaged Assessment

Student-Engaged Assessment

Strategies to Empower All Learners

Laura Greenstein
Mary Ann Burke

ROWMAN & LITTLEFIELD
Lanham • Boulder • New York • London

Published by Rowman & Littlefield
An imprint of The Rowman & Littlefield Publishing Group, Inc.
4501 Forbes Boulevard, Suite 200, Lanham, Maryland 20706
www.rowman.com

6 Tinworth Street, London, SE11 5AL, United Kingdom

Copyright © 2020 by Laura Greenstein and Mary Ann Burke

All images courtesy of pixabay.com.

All rights reserved. No part of this book may be reproduced in any form or by any electronic or mechanical means, including information storage and retrieval systems, without written permission from the publisher, except by a reviewer who may quote passages in a review.

British Library Cataloguing in Publication Information Available

Library of Congress Cataloging-in-Publication Data

Names: Greenstein, Laura, author. | Burke, Mary Ann, author.
Title: Student-engaged assessment : strategies to empower all learners / Laura Greenstein, Mary Ann Burke.
Description: Lanham, Maryland : Rowman & Littlefield, 2020. | Includes bibliographical references and index. | Summary: "Readers of this book will strengthen their knowledge and skills in selecting, designing, and using assessments that enable all learners to actively participate and monitor their own progress towards learning objectives."—Provided by publisher.
Identifiers: LCCN 2020003596 (print) | LCCN 2020003597 (ebook) | ISBN 9781475857818 (cloth) | ISBN 9781475857825 (paperback) | ISBN 9781475857832 (epub)
Subjects: LCSH: Students—Self-rating of. | Student participation in curriculum planning.
Classification: LCC LB3051 .G719 2020 (print) | LCC LB3051 (ebook) | DDC 371.26—dc23
LC record available at https://lccn.loc.gov/2020003596
LC ebook record available at https://lccn.loc.gov/2020003597

Contents

List of Figures and Tables   vii

Foreword   xi

Preface   xv

Acknowledgments   xvii

Introduction   xix

PART I

1. Foundations of Success   3
2. The SOAR Model   15
3. Touchstones of Effective Assessment   25

PART II

4. Assessment-Ready Learners   33
5. Engaging Students in Assessment   49
6. Developing Students as Owners of Assessment   69
7. When Students Become Agents of Assessment   83

PART III

8. Partnering with Parents to Empower Students   109
9. Conclusions and Next Steps   121

Bibliography	133
Index	137
About the Authors	141

Figures and Tables

FIGURES

Figure 1.1	Building blocks of success	3
Figure 1.2	Venn diagram comparing tests to assessments	9
Figure 1.3	When students own their learning	12
Figure 3.1	Assessments that lead to success	25
Figure 4.1	Success starts with the first step	33
Figure 5.1	Engage me and I learn	49
Figure 5.2	Assessments that engage learners	62
Figure 6.1	When students become owners of their own assessment	69
Figure 7.1	Walt Disney Concert Hall	83
Figure 7.2	Traditional graph	94
Figure 7.3	Student as tracker	94
Figure 8.1	Partnering with parents in support of learning	109
Figure 9.1	Essentials of student-focused assessment	122
Figure 9.2	Next steps: finding balance	124
Figure 9.3	Don't let the camel's nose into the tent	130

TABLES

Table 2.1	The SOAR Model	15
Table 2.2	SOAR Action Plan for Student Engagement	23
Table 3.1	Assessment-Readiness Lesson Design	29
Table 4.1	Reflection on Student Readiness for Assessment	40
Table 4.2	I Am Prepared to Learn and Self-Assess	41
Table 4.3	Applying SOAR to Student Readiness	44
Table 5.1	Incorporating SOAR into "SMART" Goal Setting	55
Table 5.2	Sample Personalized Learning Goals	57
Table 5.3	SOAR Analysis of Davi's SMART Goals	59
Table 5.4	Applying SOAR to Student Engagement	67
Table 6.1	Making the Transition from Engagement to Ownership	73
Table 6.2	Developing Assessment-Capable Learners	77
Table 6.3	SOAR Analysis of Sasha's Use of the Empowerment Model	79
Table 6.4	Reflection on Students' Ownership of Learning	80
Table 6.5	Developing Engaged Learners and Assessors	81
Table 7.1	SOAR Analysis of Student Agency	89
Table 7.2	Assessment Choice Board	91
Table 7.3	Weighted Choice Board	92
Table 7.4	SMART Goals in a Student's Words	95
Table 7.5	Student Reflection and Motivation	99
Table 7.6	Mindset Reflection for Students	100
Table 7.7	Accountability Rubric	101
Table 7.8	Self-Assessment of Personal Accountability	102
Table 7.9	SOAR Analysis	105

Table 8.1	Readiness of Teachers and Parents to Engage and Empower Students as Assessors	112
Table 8.2	Checklist on Strategies That Support Partnering with Parents	114
Table 8.3	Teacher Reflection on Next Steps in Partnering with Parents to Engage Students in Self-Assessment	117
Table 8.4	Parent Feedback and Reflection on Weekly Homework Assignments	118
Table 8.5	Student Reflection on How Parents Supported Their Learning on Weekly Homework Assignments	119

Foreword

According to the *Future of Jobs Report* published by the World Economic Forum (2018) educators now face a daunting task of preparing students for a future no one can predict. The key aspect of this preparation involves helping students develop adaptive skills that will enable them to adjust to these new futures as they evolve. These skills involve the abilities to understand, in a specific situation, what is required of them, where they are deficient, what they need to learn, and how to proceed with that learning.

As outlined in this report, in the near future, technology adoption will render many job skills obsolete. This obsolescence will be balanced by the creation of new jobs. These jobs will require that workers are equipped with futureproof skills such as flexible reasoning and purposeful analysis that will enable them to learn continuously.

To move forward on this daunting task, assessment becomes the focal point of educational practice. In this volume Greenstein and Burke place students—not teachers or administrators—at the center of an all-important assessment process. The authors provide specific guidelines for selecting, designing and using assessments that help students become owners of their own assessment. When students engage in the assessment processes described in this book, they will gain skills in self-reflecting on their own learning and develop strategies for self-evaluating their own performance. By engaging in this purposeful and focused assessment process—a process that the authors take care to differentiate from "testing"—students will gain the futureproof learning skills that will contribute to their adaptability in an age of rapid change.

The authors also describe specific features of effective assessments. *Student-focused assessments* offer students opportunities to personalize and adjust learning objectives. *Informative assessments* help students who may feel disenfranchised due to failures, use feedback from assessments to map learning strategies that enable them to move forward successfully. *Instructionally supportive assessments* provide timely feedback that helps students clarify misunderstandings and move forward toward their learning goals

The centerpiece of the book is a carefully developed framework called SOAR that shows educators how to integrate student-owned assessments into the routines of daily instructional practice. This integration helps students develop more complex levels of thinking. When students use the SOAR model, they identify the central ideas of a topic, pair these ideas with big-picture standards, and develop personal learning intentions. The SOAR model delineates specific step-by-step processes, templates, and examples for engaging students in assessments that are specific, visible, and actionable. The SOAR model has a foundation in five non-negotiable features of effective assessment. Assessments are aligned with curricular objectives; focused on students' learning intentions; sequenced in a step-by-step pattern; differentiated to reflect differences in students' learning plans; and are visible to everyone involved in the learning process.

The book is based on a breadth of solid research on the value of using assessment as a means of enhancing learning. In one meta-analysis of research on the effect of feedback on performance Kluger and DeNisi (1996) indicate that assessments are most effective when they create a discrepancy between a learner's sense of self-competency and the learner's performance on an assessment. When the assessment feedback does not match the individual's idealized sense of competence, the individual involved may experience a discrepancy. "Somethings wrong: I'm not as good as I thought I was." Such discrepancy-enhancing assessments can lead to performance-enhancing learning cycles when the assessment includes certain fundamental features. First, the assessment shows individuals that they are making progress toward a goal of proficiency. Next, the feedback outlines a path along with strategies for improvement. Third, the feedback links current practices with past, successful performance in a related domain. "Remember last time, when you revised your story and it more closely matched the rubric. The feedback also includes student goal setting: "Here's what I want to be able to do and here's a plan to get there." Finally, and most importantly, feedback via assessment is offered frequently. Overall, assessments encourage further learning when the feedback focuses individual's attention on the task at hand and provides specific guidance on improving performance on the task

There are also instances when assessments can lead to diminished learning and performance. In these cases, the person assessed experiences the feedback as discouraging because the information threatens their self-esteem. "Why bother? I'm simply not smart enough to do this." Assessments also impede further learning when the information is overly complex. In these situation learners may think: "I don't understand what to do next. There are 21 corrective actions listed on this assessment. Where do I start?" Overall, assessments that deter further learning shift individual's focus away from improving performance on a task at hand to an ineffective focus on themselves, their self-esteem, and, possibly, their deficiencies as learners.

Throughout their book Greenstein and Burke offer effective strategies for designing assessments that initiate a performance enhancing learning cycle. This begins with consistent, clear, and realistic standards that induce evidence of personal achievement. They then provide clear guidance on how to advance this learning cycle by using assessments to show progress, illuminate a path towards improvement, provide evidence of relationships with prior successful performance, and offer guidance on planning next steps and setting future goals. These assessment strategies also avoid the ineffective assessment-feedback cycle in which individuals focus on their own deficiencies instead of the task at hand.

The performance gaps evident in American schools would quickly dissipate if more educators followed the strategies Greenstein and Burke outline in this insightful publication.

Barry Sheckley is Professor Emeritus in the Department of Educational Leadership at the University of Connecticut. He has researched the design of educational environments that encourage students to take ownership and agency in their learning.

He has published extensively on student's self-regulated learning and instructional strategies that lead to and sustain students as owners of their learning. He is a contributing author of "Testing Too Much?: A Principal's Guide to Cutting Back Testing and Reclaiming Instructional Time."

Barry has been recognized by the Connecticut Association of Schools, The University of Connecticut Administrator Preparation Program. He has received University of Connecticut Alumni Association's Award for Excellence in Teaching; the Association of Continuing and Higher Education's Marlowe Froke Award for Excellence in Professional Writing; the American Society for Training and Development's Excellence in Research to Practice Award, and, from the Council for Experiential Education, a lifetime achievement award in recognition of his insightful contributions to the field of experiential learning.

He believes that "When you set up the opportunity for kids in a learning situation where there is not simply one right answer and they're given the freedom to exhibit their agency, they can come up with some really terrific ideas."

REFERENCES

(2018). The Future of Jobs Report 2018, Centre for the New Economy and Society.

Kluger, A. N. and A. DeNisi (1996). "The effects of feedback interventions on performance: A historical review, a meta-analysis, and a preliminary feedback intervention theory." *Psychological Bulletin* 119(2): 254-284.

Preface

Imagine you have been practicing for an upcoming concert, but when you take your seat, you find that your instrument has been reconfigured and the music is unfamiliar. Now, put yourself in Saree's seat. She has memorized the signposts on her learning path (for example, vocabulary or equations) only to discover that the path is taking her in a new direction, up a steep hill (using that vocabulary or equation in a hypothetical situation). For some, this is the worst nightmare; for others, it is the beginning of a courageous adventure.

Individual reactions to tests, measures, and evaluations rely deeply on personal experiences, perspectives, and mindsets. Can you remember a time that you prepared for a test only to discover you had studied the wrong material? Or perhaps you crammed late into the night, but when you arrived for your exam, you discovered that all you had to do was to create an acrostic using each letter of the alphabet to explain what you learned.

We are standing at a crossroads in education. Some believe that personalized, programmed instruction will raise our students' achievement. Others are enthusiastically predicting how technology will improve outcomes. But as Bill Gates acknowledged, "It would be great if our education stuff worked, but that we won't know for probably a decade" (Strauss 2013).

In education we follow the same reform pathways, anticipating better results each time. Whether the makeover is common standards, experiential learning, essential questions, career pathways, or scripted lessons, the trajectory is similar. Someone outside the classroom designs it, step-by-step sequences are followed. For the most part, the gains have been minimal, and past failings have not slowed down the reformers (Greene and McShane 2018).

> The best time to plant a tree was 20 years ago.
> The second-best time is now.
>
> —Chinese Proverb

Acknowledgments

There are countless people who made this book possible: Laura owes all of them her highest admiration and deepest appreciation. She is indebted to her writing partner, Mary Ann, who continuously inspired her and constantly urged her to "keep on keeping on" as well as to the numerous teachers and graduate students who intrepidly put these ideas into practice in schools and classrooms. Time and again, they shared their own experiences and urged us to continue down this valuable path. And special thanks go to their students, who willingly and inquisitively tried new ideas, with open minds, kind hearts, and their best efforts.

There are too many people, teams, and groups to thank individually, but we are both grateful that each was willing to share their experiences, insights, and recommendations. To name a few: the fine folks at the University of New Haven, University of Connecticut, Johnson and Wales University, the Montville and the East Lyme Public Schools, and also Fred, Dave, Jim, Kim, Steve, and Kathy, who are members of the Assessment Network Advisory Board, and especially in memory of Christine, who will be deeply missed.

We couldn't have done this without the unwavering encouragement and support from our families during the hours we spent traveling, conferencing, texting, and emailing, coast to coast. The team at Rowman & Littlefield was continuously, persistently, and amazingly supportive throughout the process.

We are also grateful to so many colleagues who opened their doors, minds, and hearts to our initiative; students who willingly took on unfamiliar challenges; and of course their families, for their enduring patience and sustained encouragement. Mary Ann could not have effectively served high-needs families without ongoing mentorships with Diana Marich, Lee Mahon, Lawrence O. Picus, Reynaldo Baca, Robb Clouse, Randolph E. Ward, Javetta Robinson, Linda Aceves, and Angelica Ramsey.

The GenParenting blogging team provides ongoing guidance and research on emerging educational issues relevant to teachers, parents, and all who care for children. These blogging leaders include Rosemarie Perez, Karen Salzer, Joyce Iwasaki, Yvette King-Berg, Jaime Koo, Danielle Gentry, and Denise Williams.

We would like to thank Julie Howard, principal of Robert Sanders K–5 Elementary School, located in east San Jose, for her ongoing support of fully engaging parents in their students' learning as self-assessors. Wanny Hersey, founding superintendent of Bullis K–8 Public Charter School located in Los Altos, inspired us with her many whole child school initiatives that support student-engaged assessments.

Yvette King-Berg, executive director of Youth Policy Institute Charter Schools (Bert Corona Charter Middle and High Schools) located in Los Angeles School District, provided countless examples of how they provide students with authentic learning experiences. Through these learning opportunities, students become academically savvy, prepared, and outwardly focused for college and careers to better serve their communities.

We are grateful to share David Hoobler's incredible copyrighted art for our book cover. David is the author and illustrator of a delightful trilogy of books on Zonk the Dreaming Tortoise. His exquisite watercolor paintings inspire children and adults to look beyond their nature observations and daily life to discover new treasures with creative insight and knowledge.

Mr. Hoobler's art can inspire teachers and students to rediscover their beliefs about learning when having students self-assess and become more fully engaged in their classroom assignments. David applies his knowledge of nature and ocean life in common core standard presentations for students at schools when sharing his books at www.Davidhoobler.com.

But above all, each of us knows that it is teachers who continue to make the biggest difference in the classroom, every day throughout the world. Thank you!

We encourage you to consider the ideas in this book, try some out, let us know how they work, and share your observations through the Assessment Network and the GenParenting websites.

Introduction

Learning is a very personal experience. Even listening to the same story may result in children offering varying summaries, comparisons, or modifications. Assessment is also a personal experience. One student may give up when they encounter a problem they cannot solve while another may skip over it. Some learners begin with a mindset of failure, others with a belief they are capable of anything.

At the same time that students bring different experiences, beliefs, and attributes to the classroom, the qualities of best practice in assessment are consistent. One of the best resources from the National Academies Press, *Knowing What Students Know: The Science and Design of Educational Assessment*, is freely available online (https://www.nap.edu/catalog/10019/knowing-what-students-know-the-science-and-design-of-educational). There's also a wealth of information on the best practices in student self-assessment. Many books explain strategies to use in the classroom. For this book, we decided to start at the end—with why engaging students in assessment is essential for students' lifelong learning—then figuring out the best ways to engage them.

> Tell me and I'll forget. Show me and I may remember. Involve me and I learn.
>
> —Benjamin Franklin

This book is about selecting, designing, and using assessments that enable all students to be successful. For some, this means mastering test-taking strategies. For others, it means focusing the assessment lens on the process of learning rather than emphasizing final outcomes. Learning aims and intentions are best accomplished by maximizing student engagement in assessment through transparency, voice, and choice.

We relied on Abraham Maslow's recognition that students must feel safe and supported in school before they can begin to deconstruct educational objectives into actionable learning intentions that are accompanied by clear success criteria. Readiness means that students can make connections to their own worldview and life experiences, and that there are opportunities to personalize assessment and place the emphasis on progress rather than scores. Thus, the first section of the book looks at ways to develop these essential foundations.

> We do not learn from experience. We learn from reflecting on experience.
>
> —John Dewey

The book also reinforces the idea that it is the student who must be at the center of assessment. Engagement is essential, and guidance must be available on personalizing learning goals and developing an action plan for learning and assessing. This may include asking students for their input on what should be measured to including them in the design of the assessment.

The next step is helping students become owners of assessment: where responsibility begins to shift from teacher to student. This means students know what and why they are learning and also develop skills to self-monitor their steps in relation to their learning intentions.

Students as agents of assessment can align their learning intentions and actions with the outcomes of their learning. They rely on feedback and revision for improving their outcomes and increasingly have choice and voice in displaying their learning.

The book also emphasizes the importance of self-reflection and reliance on feedback. Metacognition is strengthened as they think about their learning, process, products, and outcomes. Mindsets adjust from seeing assessment as a finality to seeing it as an ongoing dialogue.

Throughout the book, the authors share their experiences in ways that can be intentionally and advantageously used to help all students succeed. It grew out of their shared passion for teaching and learning, and developed into a powerful belief—built on the voices, research, and evidence of many—that increasing student engagement in assessment can improve learning outcomes.

THINK ABOUT IT

Every learner brings their own set of expectations and needs to learning. Take a moment to assess your own skills and knowledge in developing assessment-capable learners:

- Novice: I am just starting to learn about this. I don't really understand it yet.
- Apprentice: I am starting to understand, but not quite ready to work independently yet.
- Practitioner: I can mostly do this by myself, but sometimes I get stuck and need some help.
- Expert: I understand it fully and can explain or demonstrate the concept to someone else.

Then

1. Write a note to yourself, explaining what you want or need to learn more about.
2. Think about the steps, processes, or resources you need to move forward on your journey.

Part I

Chapter One

Foundations of Success

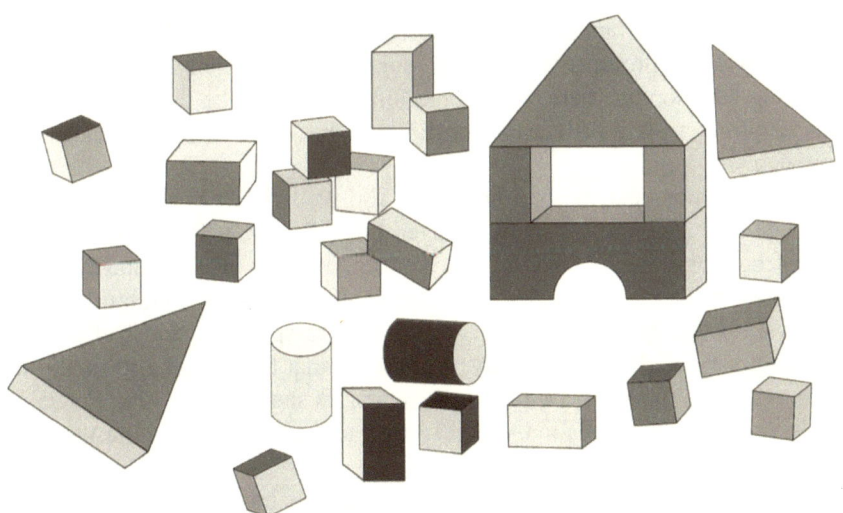

Figure 1.1. Building blocks of success

> The objective of education is to prepare the young to educate themselves throughout their lives.
>
> —Robert Maynard Hutchins

What is it that leads to educational achievement and success in life? The question has no simple answers and opens a Pandora's box of more questions. First, the concepts of competency and success can have different meanings. Additionally, educational achievement may look different in different settings. For example, it can mean mastering basic skills in one place and a complex mixture of abstract ideas and innovative thinking in others. The same goes for success: It can be viewed from a personal, family, or career perspective. To some, it means overcoming obstacles or sustaining meaningful relationships, to others, profitable entrepreneurship.

This book will focus on the groundwork of success for all students. Special attention will be given to those beliefs, habits, and underpinnings that prepare students to be insightful self-assessors throughout their lives. The reader will find information on the skill and knowledge, and strategies necessary for accurate self-assessment. Many can easily and immediately be implemented in schools and classrooms. Others are worth a little more time and practice to develop by both students and teachers.

If children are to be successful, they must first feel safe and supported. Maslow (1943) taught us this through his hierarchy of needs. Yet, for some learners, life is not safe. They may live in crime-ridden neighborhoods where it's not safe to walk home from school. Others are chronically hungry. A student named Jake qualified for free/reduced lunches, but his mother was too proud to accept help. Jake would routinely show up at the learning lab, hoping there were some leftovers from the day's snack. The teacher always put a little aside for him, and he was always appreciative in his own shy way.

By his junior year, he had taken and did well on ASVAB (the military aptitude test) and enrolled in the Delayed Entry Program. Two years after his high school graduation, he returned to his school to tell his story and thank his teachers, counselors, and especially the principal who mentored him through the process. He was proud of his promotion to specialist and had already earned a service ribbon. Privately, he told me that he was glad to finally be able to pay his mother back for all the sacrifices she made for him. For Jake, building foundations of food, medical care, and stability in his life were essential foundations for success.

Well-being in assessment comes when students have a clear understanding of the learning intentions and also have opportunities to personalize and adjust them in ways that make sense to them and support their success. This may mean deconstructing large-scale standards into actionable and measurable interim steps. For example, "Compare two decimals by reasoning about their size" (CCSS Math 4.NF.C.7) becomes "I can read and understand decimals and put them in order." When Carlita is asked which answer is true (A) $0.7 > 0.4$ or (B) $0.4 > 0.7$, she becomes apprehensive when she can't remember what the $<$ and $>$ symbols mean. Fortunately, when her teacher posts, $>$ means is greater than, she has an aha moment and completes the task accurately.

Once learners' needs for safety and well-being are met and they feel academically and emotionally secure in their classroom, *inclusion and belonging* is another step toward personal achievement. Standardized tests are mandatory, but they may not sustain these basic needs for struggling learners. This book will preview classroom techniques that do. This includes assessments that are inclusive of all learners, routinely incorporated within teaching and learning, relevant to the student, aligned with learning, and comprehensive in their use of a spectrum of methods and actions that support progress toward mastery.

Informative assessment is essential for all students, especially those who may feel disenfranchised or have experienced failure. Instructionally supportive assessment relies on frequent check-ins for understanding as well as feedback that provides clarification on misunderstandings and guidance on next steps. These assessments give learners voice, such as adding annotations to their responses or asking lingering questions within the assessment. Feedback can come from teachers as well as peers with these prompts: "What you said about ___ is very clear, but I'm still confused on ___," or "I see you included ___ but have you also thought about ___?"

As students mature, they develop clearer ideas about who they are and how they think. They begin to recognize their strengths as well as struggles. This development of *self-awareness and self-esteem* can be fostered by assessments that encourage and guide students in monitoring their learning. When students become reflective and flexible assessors, they can also personalize learning intentions. For example, when given a choice in showing understanding of event sequences, Wei decides to make an instructive video on writing a graphic novel, while Fiona wants to illustrate a user's guide to sustainable gardens.

One day, Max said to his teacher, "I want to try something new for my project, but don't want to be penalized for lack of creativity, since it's the first time I'm using Piktochart, an infographic maker." After a brief conversation, they mutually agreed to count the content ratings of the rubric at 80 percent and the design ratings at 20 percent. With the pressure off, Max was inspired to try a new way to show his learning. In all these examples, consistency and clarity of learning objectives are central to success.

There are numerous student-owned elements of assessment that have been shown to increase success. These include:

- clarity of purpose
- relevance to the learner
- authentic experiences

- personalized meaning
- purposeful reflection
- informative feedback
- gauges of progress
- reliance on coherent assessments and measurements

A good place to begin is by translating big-picture ideas into local actions.

FROM BIG-PICTURE STANDARDS TO LOCAL ASSESSMENT: BECOMING PROACTIVE

There are thousands of Common Core State Standards (CCSS) for students to master from kindergarten through twelfth grade in English language arts (ELA), math, science, social studies, arts, career and technical education, and more. Teacher evaluations are often based on their students' achievement of these academic standards. In reality, the standards are generally too broad for both students and teachers. For example, third graders are expected to "Explain the function of nouns, pronouns, verbs, adjectives, and adverbs in general and their functions in particular sentences" (L.3.1.a).

Seventh graders will "Solve multi-step mathematical problems posed with positive and negative rational numbers in any form (whole, fractions, decimals) using tools strategically and apply properties of operations to calculate with numbers in any form; convert between forms as appropriate; assess the reasonableness of answers using mental computation and estimation strategies" (7.EE.3).

From the start, teachers, students, parents, and communities must have clarity of what learners are expected to know and do. They cannot wait for test results after the learning cycle is over or the school year has ended to learn about students' achievement. Even interim assessments may come weeks after instruction on a particular learning outcome. By then the opportunity for student self-reflection and modifications to learning may come too late and be less effective. Cognitive research shows that immediate feedback is more effective in changing thinking and guiding improvement than delayed test scores (Stenger, 2014).

Being proactive means being preventative or averting problems. It is at the local level that students and teachers can be proactive by translating big-picture outcomes into local goals and short-term learning steps. Proactive also means taking responsibility for your decisions and your actions. Introduce this idea by asking students about their experiences getting caught in a rainstorm or unintentionally breaking something: Have them think about what could have prevented it. Then talk about being proactive in school, by asking for help on a specific stumbling point or helping classmates, who are on the verge of tearing up their paper or throwing their tablet across the room.

When Garth had difficulty sorting words into verbs or adjectives, Rosie showed her list to him and explained that adjectives describe things. She demonstrated her understanding by stating that furry describes a dog and beautiful describes a hat. Rosie then clarified that verbs are action words such as speak, ran, feel. She stated, "I know it can be confusing when you have to decide if confuse or confused is a verb, but I don't think that is on our list. Let me know if you need more help." This simple act of helping another is an important part of engaging and empowering students as assessors.

Proactive assessment is more timely, focused, and actionable than benchmark and summative measures. It relies on self-reflection in relation to learning intentions as well as self-reliance in responding to informative feedback. Proactive assessment engages students in explaining what they learned, comparing it to their goals, identifying lingering questions, and making recommendations for next steps. In relation to improving learning outcomes, a proactive mindset is ready to face the unexpected. Anton explains that "the review sheet made me realize that I skipped the third stage. I reviewed what we learned and corrected my work. Now, I think my grade should change from 79 to 84."

STUDENTS AT THE CENTER

In the course of reading this book, you will find examples, descriptions, and case studies of the best practices for developing assessment-capable learners. It is in the classroom, moment by moment, day by day, that teachers and students can check for understanding and track progress toward targets with more accuracy than periodic tests. It is also in the classroom that students can monitor learning, make adjustments, and track steps toward success.

It is essential to keep the student at the center of assessment. For example, if multiple types of assessments are used for instructional purposes, then they must be made specific to the standards yet responsive to the student. In doing so, the needs of individual learners can be accommodated, allowing some to go deeper and others to work on basic mastery. The motivational value of assessment is enhanced by in-the-moment feedback, whether from the teacher, peers, or a computer program. Relevant and engaging tasks combined with embedded formative assessment can incentivize students to move toward finding answers and solutions.

Andrade, Huff, and Brooke (2012) summarize this well when they point out that being student focused means centering on students' strengths, needs, and interests; promoting learning through growth; involving students in setting goals; monitoring progress; and determining how to address any gaps (2).

Keep in mind that caution must be taken when using any assessment for too many purposes. "One of the truisms in educational measurement is that when an assessment system is designed to fulfill too many purposes—especially disparate purposes—it rarely fulfills any purpose well" (Perie, Marion, Gong, and Wurtzel, 2007, 6). Thus, the balance of standardized assessment, formative assessment, and self-assessment can provide valuable information for multiple purposes and users.

Blending transitioning/evolving external tests with internal assessments results in these practices:

- Assessment happens at the classroom and learner level (rather than whole-school measures).
- It is done with the learners (rather than done to them).
- Learners are recognized for their progress toward mastery (rather than comparisons to others).
- Assessment takes on many forms (rather than predetermined communal methods).
- It continuously evolves toward personalized methods (rather than standardized time, place, and process).

Students taking an assessment during their teacher preparation program were asked to compare and contrast the terms *test* and *assessment*: Explain how they each have unique qualities and uses and in what ways they have a common meaning and application. They work in small groups. Some prepare a list; others illustrate their ideas.

One group explains that a test is primarily a measure of knowledge. It provides data to help teachers select resources or sort students into learning groups. They add that assessment measures more than a test does and can have more uses than a test.

When they are finished, they are given figure 1.2 to identify ways in which their responses aligned with the diagram. They are also asked to identify gaps or disparities and explain how they would adjust, improve, or elaborate their responses.

These basic comparisons will be explored more deeply throughout this book. Part I introduces the main ideas of student-centered and student-engaged assessment. In Part II you will find specific strategies for preparing, engaging, and empowering students as assessors. In Part III you will be asked

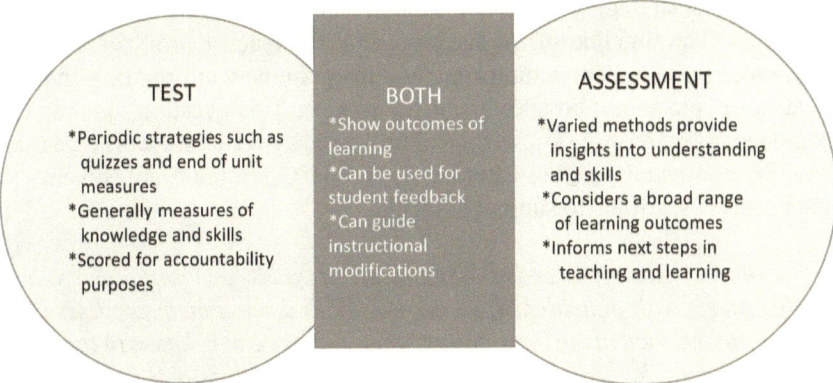

Figure 1.2. Venn diagram comparing tests to assessments

to consider your next steps and chart your own path. Dylan Wiliam (2018) at Learning Sciences International describes testing as an event and assessment as a process.

Think about It: Reflection and Analysis of Understanding Testing and Assessment

Think about these typical test questions from a teacher certification exam. They are borrowed from the Indiana Core Assessments for Educator Licensure. Questions 1 and 2 include explanations of the thinking behind the correct responses. Question 3 asks for your analysis of the question and the choice of responses.

Question 1: In which of the following situations is a teacher most clearly applying the concept of scaffolding to promote student learning?

A. A middle school mathematics teacher allows students to discontinue independent practice of a new skill once they have correctly solved three problems in a row.
B. A high school English teacher offers students a choice of three articles to read and summarize as part of an interdisciplinary unit on the Renaissance.
C. A middle school science teacher directs students to write down each step of an experiment on identifying acids and bases as they perform it.
D. A high school world history teacher reviews and posts a timeline of key world events to provide students with a context for analyzing about events and factors leading up to the Korean conflict.

Correct response: D

Scaffolding strategies are used to support students' learning of new content and skills. The timeline of events posted by the teacher provides students with a tool to help them comprehend and integrate new information and understand its place in a broader historical context. This question requires the examinee to demonstrate knowledge of processes by which students construct meaning and acquire skills. Choices A, B, and C are more adjustments to practice than scaffolds to support students.

Question 2: During extended assignments, a middle school language arts teacher meets with individual students weekly to discuss their progress. The teacher guides students in considering where they are in relation to the overall assignment, identifies what is going well, and develops a plan to address aspects of the project that are particularly challenging. This reflective process is likely to be particularly useful for promoting which of the following outcomes?

A. Reducing students' tendency to evaluate their academic performance in relation to that of their peers
B. Helping students develop the habit of applying standard criteria to their work
C. Supporting students in becoming independent learners who take responsibility for their own learning
D. Ensuring that students place a high priority on academic achievement

Correct response: C

When students are routinely encouraged and guided in reflecting on their learning and progress, they begin to recognize areas of strength, interest, and needs. This recognition helps them manage their own learning. During their meetings, the teacher is leading students through a transferrable process that they can apply to their learning both in and outside of school. This question requires the examinee to demonstrate an understanding of ways to promote students' organizational and time-management skills and build a sense of responsibility for their own learning.

Question 3. In Paragraph 6 of the source document, why did the author use the word "test" rather than "assessment"?

A. *Assessment* has a different intention and meaning than the term *test*.
B. The author was describing different types of questions.

C. A test implies a broader interpretation of the term *assessment*.
D. The author was referring to a strategy for quantifying learning.

Correct response: D, but what if the learner selected C?

What does that show about the candidates' understanding? What clarification and deeper understandings do they need? Recommend a better or more valid way to check the learners' understanding.

If that activity caused you to think about your beliefs and practices, you are in the right place to learn more. In this book you will be introduced to these four key ideas of student-engaged assessment and become familiar with strategies for translating them into practice:

1. Preparing students to be assessment ready
2. Engaging learners in assessment
3. Conveying ownership and responsibility for assessment
4. Empowering students as agents of their own assessment

WHEN STUDENTS OWN THEIR LEARNING

We live in an era of extreme headlines and excessive claims about what works in education. Headline writers know that emotional messages draw people's attention. Consider these examples: "Social-Emotional Learning Gears Up for Artificial Intelligence" or "Tremendous Migration to Self-Directed Learning." Neither of these claims have valid research behind them. The practice of students as self-assessors and as agents of assessments is relatively new.

There is emerging research on the importance of engaging learners in assessment. A meta-analysis by Panadero, Jonsson, and Botella (2017) showed positive effects of self-assessment on self-regulation and self-efficacy (a belief in oneself to overcome obstacles and achieve goals). A study at Stanford (Bae and Kokka, 2016) found that engagement led to meaningful learning, increased autonomy, and more accurate self-assessment. In addition, Taylor and Parsons (2011) made the important distinction that engagement is being redefined from focusing on disengaged learners to emphasizing practices that engage all learners.

Think about how Matthew Lynch (2018) summarizes the value of students' owning their learning in figure 1.3. Based on your own experiences, what do you agree or disagree with? Are there concepts you would add or delete?

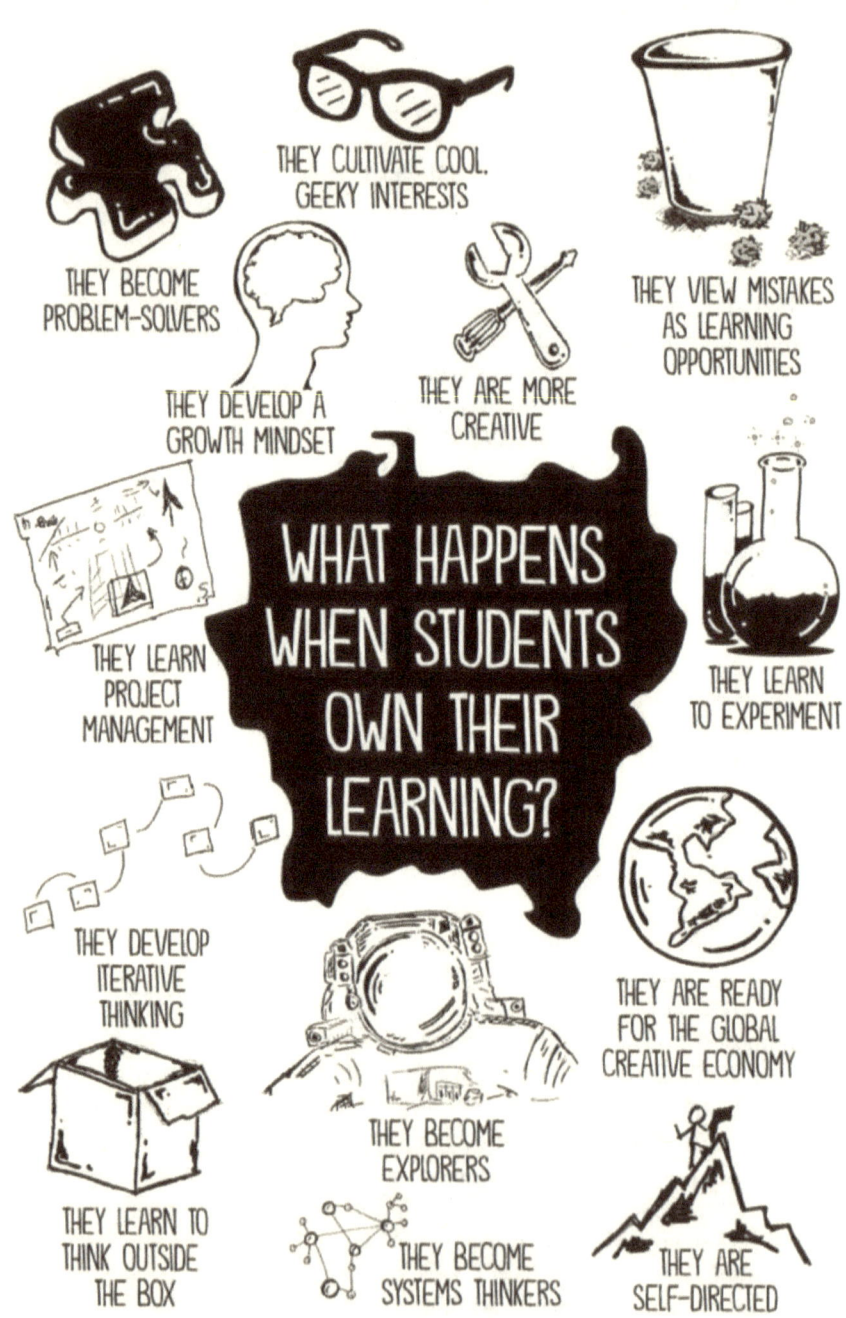

Figure 1.3. When students own their learning

LOCAL APPLICATION OF LEARNING

With your teaching team, reflect on the following statements:

- Consider and identify your students' needs.
- What knowledge and skills do you have/need to support these needs?
- Define your school's expectations for developing and engaging students as self-assessors.

What is MY TEAM'S experience with engaging and empowering students as assessors?

What are OUR STUDENTS' NEEDS AND EXPECTATIONS in relation to assessment?

Describe your SCHOOL/DISTRICT REQUIREMENTS AND POLICIES about testing and assessment.

What are your LINGERING QUESTIONS and FIRST STEPS for developing assessment-capable learners?

What are the current OPPORTUNITIES for developing assessment-capable learners?

What are the CONSTRAINTS?

Chapter Two

The SOAR Model

While developing the ideas in this book, clearly defined activities emerged for engaging and supporting students as self-assessors. Turning the fundamentals of student-centered assessment into practice led to the design of *SOAR: Student Ownership and Agency Leads to Results*. In table 2.1 the original designations are shown in italics, but as our ideas developed, we recognized other important elements and included them in each category of SOAR.

Table 2.1. The SOAR Model

Acronym	Indicates/ Represents	In Practice
S	*Student Standards* Strategies	From the start, *students* understand how big-picture standards lead to local and personal learning intentions. They begin to visualize and plan the *strategies, sequences,* and *structures* that make learning assessable and sustainable.
O	*Ownership* Onus Organization	Students take *ownership* and responsibility (*onus*) for designing, *organizing*, and personalizing learning and assessment. Relying on *opportunities* and support, they develop plans that are well defined, feasible, and actionable.
A	*Agency* Accountability Achievement	As students become *agents* of learning and assessment, their interest and attentiveness increase. Perseverance and *accountability* lead to higher levels of *achievement*, insightful self-assessment, and modifications to learning.
R	*Results* Review Response	Results of student ownership and agency are evident in learning outcomes, *results*, and mindful *reflections*. Students are increasingly willing to *review, reassess,* and *responsively* modify outcomes with an emphasis on improvement.

SOAR represents the integration of student-engaged and student-owned assessment into the routines of daily practice. It is not an add-on to teaching but rather guides the structure and cadence of learning. It supports students' progress, informs instruction, and leads to meaning and success in schools.

It is also important to keep in mind that the practices that develop student agency are not something new, but rather rely on a trajectory of enduring ideas. They emerge from theory, research, and best practice from human development, educational psychology, the learning sciences, and research on assessment. In this model, agency isn't conveyed but rather is the result of learning, evidence, reflection, and accountability.

REACHING HIGHER WITH SOAR

When students in a teacher preparation program were asked to explain the difference between digging deeper and reaching higher in learning, they reflected, collaborated, and proposed that digging deeper into learning means gathering more information and evaluating and making judgments about the value, relevance, and accuracy of the information. Reaching higher refers to attaining higher levels of thinking in a taxonomical sequence of learning. Whether you choose Benjamin Bloom's, Norman Webb's, SOLO, or other sequences of learning, it doesn't matter. What matters is that learners stretch upward to higher levels of inquiry, analysis, constructing ideas, and generating artifacts.

In the SOAR model, the student is reaching toward more complex levels of thinking. It is no longer acceptable for students to simply define the vocabulary in a reading, sequence the battles of Gettysburg, or memorize the periodic table. Increasingly, the emphasis is on how well students understand the meaning and significance of their learning. Do they have opportunities for transferring ideas to other settings and situations? For younger learners, it's what happens when they are asked why a character did something rather than describing the character's appearance. It means going beyond just naming a shape and having students cut a single piece of paper into five triangles. It's what happens when you pair *I Robot*, *The Hunger Games*, or *Day after Tomorrow*, with current events and authenticated facts to guide and inform students on scientifically based predictions for the future.

SOAR also encourages deeper learning. This means exploring learning through multiple lenses to uncover the complex intricacies of learning. For younger children, it is not only attending a field trip to a bee farm, but thinking about what would happen if there were no longer bees in the world. Or perhaps, learning about dinosaurs and then creating a dinosaur that could live in today's environment. Deeper learning helps students recognize that straightforward information often has weightier and broader meanings—and that it can be fun and creative to delve into these ideas.

When students in Ms. Em's fifth-grade class were asked to think about a world with no bees, Aman said, "That would be great, because my sister is allergic." Amira added, "But, I would really miss honey on my peanut butter sandwich." Ms. Em explained the importance of bees in pollination and then asked students to imagine a world without whales, or hate, or even teachers.

As students use the SOAR model, they begin by identifying the central ideas of a topic, pair these with big-picture standards, develop local learning intentions, and then plan and personalize those aims and goals. In the past, all the students would have watched a video, gone on a field trip, or invited an expert such as a beekeeper to visit the class to talk about pollination and the production of honey.

In a SOAR classroom, students demonstrate their understanding of the broad learning intentions. For example, students can explain the life stages of the honey bee, the construction of their hives, how bees communicate, their role in pollination, and the production and uses of honey. They can then choose a path and strategy for further learning. Marcella prefers to work solo and wants to create a precise diagram of the inside of a hive. Chester and Deshi want to work together to present the stages of a honey bee's life. Chara wants to do "something" with honey but isn't sure yet. She begins by exploring the source, types, nutrients, and uses of honey. Each student or group then develops and describes their purposes and strategies for learning. They also consider how they can show what they learned and have it assessed in relation to their learning purposes.

In the SOAR model, each step includes specific and intentional learning actions and also how each action and outcome will be assessed. This doesn't mean there is a quiz after each step, but rather there is tracking of learning, narratives, reflections, and evidence. The SOAR model begins and ends with the students. It seamlessly conveys ownership of learning, as students monitor their progress, adjust the processes, and display their evidence of learning.

RELEASING THE POWER OF SOAR

The usefulness of SOAR comes from its potential to engage students. There is evidence that through authentic learning, supported practice, and personalization, students are more comfortable, engaged, and motivated to learn (Dyer, 2015). SOAR's emphasis on involving all learners is relevant and also essential for success in today's learning environments, instructional requirements, and students' expectations (McMillan and Hearn, 2008).

SOAR can help all learners succeed: from those who are striving to master the basics to those who are ready to take flight; and even for those who want to take off, but need more flight guidance. Self-assessment includes traditional and alternative measures through all levels of learning taxonomies. It is most effective when students know the learning intentions, have choice in displaying their learning process and outcomes, and can emphasize growth and improvement over final scores. As with all assessments, it is about balance: finding the sweet spot between the oncoming ball and the student's control of the bat.

Complex yet Practical

The complexity of assessment and especially the development of students as assessors is streamlined by the SOAR model. Each student brings a unique set of abilities, preferences, backgrounds, and beliefs. But when students share common learning intentions that are deconstructed and made relevant through personalization, learning becomes user friendly, allowing each learner to make personal connections. When students can visualize learning, develop their own pathways, and monitor progress, then the complexity, depth, and relevance of standards become more understandable, actionable, and achievable.

When Marcella's teacher helps her understand the standard that says "Recognize volume as an attribute of solid figures and understand the concept of volume measurement," she realizes it means using the length, width, and height dimensions of a rectangular pyramid to calculate its volume. Equally confusing for Sal is the standard that says "Trace and evaluate the argument and specific claims in a text, distinguishing claims that are supported by reasons and evidence from claims that are not." Ms. Em says it just means that as you read this article, decide what the author is trying to persuade you to believe and also the quality of the resources and experts the author is relying on to support his claim and reasoning.

When Jaycee learns she can pick one aspect of climate change, she gets excited about glacier melt because her grammy lives in Alaska. Developing student enthusiasm for a topic does spur interest, but it is the SOAR model that translates interest and curiosity into standards-based action.

Standards-Based yet Flexible

Today's classrooms are standards-based places. Learning begins with large-scale standards (i.e., reading for information, solving real-world mathematical problems, planning and constructing explanations, and developing solutions).

In relation to the honey bee project, those types of large-scale standards are too broad. They need to be customized so that students can understand the purpose and fine-tune their own learning intentions. Here are some examples:

- Reading for information is the foundation for identifying parts of a honeybee or illustrating their life cycle.
- Solving real-world problems can mean planning design specifications for a beehive or a garden that supports pollinators.
- In science, constructing explanations and designing solutions for vanishing bee populations leads to predicting a world without bees and proposing ways to prevent that from happening.
- Social studies standards can be used to explain how a hive is a culture and each type of bee has a specific role.
- Mapping the places in the world where bees are increasing and decreasing can lead to problem solving.
- Reading materials can be as diverse as the straightforward *Flight of the Honey Bee* by Raymond Huber, *The Case of the Vanishing Bees* by Sandra Markle, or for older students, the multilayered *The History of Bees* by Maja Lunde.

Formative *and* Informative but *not* Final

In the SOAR model, ownership and agency are directly linked to results and outcomes. For the most part, the outcomes of learning are formative in providing insights into learning and informative in guiding the next steps.

Chara sees that "integrating information from several sources" means that she will begin by researching her topic using books in the school library as well as digital resources. She is astounded to learn that there are hundreds of flavors and colors of honey depending on their source. She personalizes the big-picture standard into her own goal of learning how to infuse flavors directly into honey. She tries orange and rose petal infusions, then realizes she is developing an enthusiastic customer base from her tasting audience.

She meets her learning intention by designing an infographic on the flavors of honey in which she explains honey production and natural varieties of honey. After receiving feedback from peers, she modifies her design for infused honey to provide a clearer sequence along with specific suggestions for infusing honey at home. Using formative assessment during learning, and summative assessment at the conclusion, she is excited about her opportunities for further learning and perhaps entrepreneurship.

Precise yet Personalized

From these examples, you can see how student-engaged assessment can be specific to learning intentions and success criteria while being customizable and flexible. It's not difficult to stretch beyond traditional standards and assessment methods such as quizzes that ask students to define vocabulary or to sequence the life cycle of bees. Higher-level thinking such as critical thinking can be self-assessed using a rubric. Self-reflection of problem-solving skills can rely on an annotated checklist of the steps. Alternatively, students can design and create products such as an "Illustrated Guide to Honeybees" that aligns with the content standards and student learning intentions and also includes an assessment for the audience to complete.

Students can personalize the assessment by accompanying their presentations with Post-it Notes where the audience shares their feedback on paper or electronically. For review, they can "pass the page" (using paper or an electronic version) where students start at the bottom of a sheet of paper. Step 1 has the students describe their learning outcome. Step 2 instructs the students to fold the paper an inch or so up from the bottom and pass it along to the next person who repeats Steps 1 and 2. Then the presenter unfolds the paper, reads the summaries, and confirms or clarifies responses. Alternatively, teachers can create an empty outline where students insert specified vocabulary into the correct spaces for the teacher or presenter to review. Personalization of learning is important, but precision in assessment is essential.

Balanced yet Impartial

Assessment can be unfair to some learners. Some may understand the content but not have the language skills to explain them clearly. Others, who have experienced trauma, distress, and anxiety, may not be emotionally ready to face a nerve-wracking test. SOAR moves the meter to the fairer side of the equation. It provides a choice of strategies and multiple opportunities for displaying learning. Oscar may prefer to stay at school after dismissal to work on his model because it is quieter and has fewer distractions than at home. Chara wants to take her reading material home where she finds it more comfortable and less noisy than the classroom. When visible evidence of learning is ongoing, it is essential and feasible to continuously monitor progress rather than wait for summative test results.

With SOAR, students can rely on their strengths for displaying and sharing learning. This means that Anika can get on her soapbox and advocate for her position while Jan can quietly present his Prezi with a more reserved personal style. Aaron says that "Presenting in front of an audience is not my strong point, but I am going to give it a try today. Please focus your assessment on the information and provide feedback to help me be a more effective presenter."

Think about It: Self-Reflection of Students as Assessors

Consider these questions about student ownership and agency in general. Of course, there are emerging developmental differences from preschool to adulthood. However, these questions are intended to be more general. You are invited to adjust them and reflect on them as they are relevant to your setting.

1. *Which of the following is NOT an indicator of student ownership and agency in assessment?*

   A. Students are attentive and focused during learning and assessing.
   B. Students get good grades on their assignments and assessments.
   C. Students are curious about learning more.

   Correct response: B

   Students become engaged and interested in learning when the subject or process captures their attention. As students delve into a topic and develop more interest, they may seek more information and resources. It may challenge them to think more deeply. However, good grades can be based on other factors, such as prior knowledge or ability to learn from reading and viewing. Good grades don't always mean the student is engaged and accountable for their learning.

2. *Ms. Omarin began using grade-level lesson plans from her district's curriculum director. She likes that the lessons support the standards, are clearly sequenced, and include hands-on activities. But she notices that an important aspect of engagement seemed to be missing. Which one of these is it?*

   A. Lesson plans included background information for the teacher.
   B. Students are busy in their learning.
   C. Routine use of formative and informative assessments monitor student understanding.

   Correct response: C

It's wonderful to observe a classroom where children are actively engaged in learning. But it is more important to know whether they understand the learning. Insights from embedded formative assessments bring to light concepts and procedures that may remain confusing for the learner and also guide re-teaching, interventions, and modifications so that all students can be successful.

NEXT STEPS

Chapter 4 clarifies that when *students are assessment ready*, they understand the learning objectives. They see how big picture standards are deconstructed into *actionable learning intentions*. In this way, meaningful and *aligned learning strategies* are used to their fullest potential. This is the first step in students becoming active participants in learning and assessing.

In chapter 5, you'll find insights and practices to help *students become owners, organizers, and participants* in planning, learning, and assessing. This is where they learn how to follow and *complete sequences for learning and begin to take responsibility* for their learning. They also partner with teachers and peers in developing their assessment skills.

Chapter 6 shines a light on learning outcomes and helps students clarify any lingering sticking points or hurdles in learning and assessing. As they develop as *accountable agents, mediators, and motivators*, they begin to understand the connections between clarity in purpose and conscientiousness in action, with achievement.

In chapter 7 you will learn about steps, processes, and strategies for transferring ownership for assessment to students. This is where they *plan* the process, *monitor* their learning, have *choice* in displaying learning, and transition from traditional tests to authentic *demonstrations* of learning.

Throughout, you can explore how these ideas lead to focused responses that guide progress and improvement toward goals. In the conclusions, you can review the positive outcomes of this process for preparing, engaging, and empowering students as assessors.

Table 2.2. SOAR Action Plan for Student Engagement

Review this list of indicators of assessments that are visible, actionable, and engaging for students. Think about what is most important in your setting, then rank your selections from level 1, meaning most essential, to level 2, of moderate importance, and 3, to put on reserve for now. Annotate your rankings as relevant to your setting and situation; examples are included. Compare your thoughts to those in your professional learning team. Begin to consider ways to use the collaborative results as a guide to your implementation plan that begins with your collective level 1 steps.

SUPPORTING Student Engagement, Ownership, and Agency	TAKING ACTION on the Indicators
STUDENTS 1. *Deconstruct* large-scale standards into local goals and learning intentions that guide students in planning their learning. 2. *Verify* that students understand the learning intentions.	 Level 1: We will have students state the objectives in their own words and make connections to them throughout their learning.
3. *Illustrate* ways that students can think about sequences, structures, and strategies for learning. **OWNERSHIP** 4. *Support* students in developing well-defined, feasible, and actionable plans for learning and assessing. 5. *Provide examples and structures* that lead to the transfer of ownership and responsibility for learning and assessing to students.	
AGENCY 6. *Engage* students as self-assessors throughout teaching and learning. 7. *Responsively* build on students' strengths as well as lingering gaps in support of improvement.	2. Develop a vade mecum with strategies and procedures for students.
RESULTS 8. *Students continuously monitor and gauge* outcomes of learning, noting progress and improvements in learning. 9. *Utilize and report on multiple measures* of a spectrum of learning outcomes.	 3. We can begin in our own classrooms and will share this with leadership to see how we can incorporate this in school-wide practices.
10. *Confirm* that assessments are *flexible, fair* (without bias), *valid* (measures intended targets), and *reliable* (consistent and free of errors). **Add Your Own:**	

NOTE: The authors' numbering of items does not connote sequences, priorities, or mandates. They are included only to facilitate discussion.

Think about It: Insights and Guidance on Applying Your Learning

Throughout this book, you will find step-by-step processes, templates, and examples for engaging learners in assessment, transferring responsibility to students, encouraging ownership through opportunity, and developing students' self-assessment skills. Plan on returning to these initial reflections. Then, as you continue reading, add your own personalized indicators, make notes on ways to implement your ideas, adjust priorities, and translate concepts into personal practice.

Chapter Three

Touchstones of Effective Assessment

Figure 3.1. Assessments that lead to success

SOAR is based on decades of expertise and research on effective assessment processes that strengthen, reinforce, and sustain learning. These approaches not only measure final outcomes but also support students' understanding of the purposes of learning, encourage higher-level thinking, and increase student buy-in. All of this results in dynamic self-assessors who are willing and able to boost learning and improve outcomes.

Think about this: If we know what the best practices are in assessment, why aren't they consistently/steadfastly used? The answer is that distractions from teaching and learning are numerous and frequent. Here are some examples.

FIRST, MINIMIZE THE DISTRACTIONS

Resource swapping and frequent changes are intended to accelerate and improve learning outcomes; however, they actually decelerate learning. Consider the time it takes to learn to teach from a new curriculum, master a new student management program, become proficient using new technologies and new "texts," start new schedules, and more. These routine distractions can sidetrack teaching, resulting in diminished learning.

Bright shiny "things" that claim to result in miraculous improvement are often singularities. Whether it be persuasive marketing or claims of extraordinary progress, it's wise to dig deeper into the source and research process, as well as the analysis and presentation of data. Remember that when asked about the Common Core Standards, Bill Gates responded by saying *"It would be great if our education stuff worked, but that we won't know for probably a decade"* (Strauss, 2013). By 2010, forty-one states adopted the Common Core, and by 2013, states began to rescind their adoption.

Continually changing standards, learning goals, objectives, targets, and intentions are stressful. As evidenced by that list, we no longer share a common vocabulary for learning outcomes. Imagine if you returned home to a rearranged kitchen every day. It takes a period of adjustment to get comfortable with the setup, find the materials you need, and learn how to use the appliances to produce edible outcomes.

With all the talk of teaching students to separate fact from fiction, it's just as important for educators to be able to distinguish validated evidence from unsubstantiated assertions. Instead of assessment distractions, it's better to rely on the explicit and steady practices that are proven to work. These approaches reduce the anxiety that comes from frequent changes and lift learners to higher levels of achievement. However, these changes must be effective, proven, verified, validated, confirmed, and authenticated, not just endorsed by a well-known/renowned source.

Rather than repeat past missteps, the authors relied on a synthesis of best practices that have endured over time and across settings, programs, and frameworks, with learners who are alike as well as dissimilar.

ASSESSMENT THAT LEADS TO SUCCESS

Focus on these five nonnegotiables of assessment:

1. *Aligned:* There is visible alignment between standards, curriculum, learning intentions, lesson design, and assessment. Instructional processes are purposefully planned to support learning.

Questions to consider: What and why are you assessing this? What's the purpose and how is this conveyed to students? In what ways is this mutually responsive and supportive?

2. *Student focused:* Maintains a focus on students. There is evidence that they understand the sequence and strategies for learning. Real-world challenges capture attention and sustain deeper learning. Exemplars and resources are presented or provided.

   Questions to Consider: What do they need to know, understand, and do? How can they best learn, transfer and apply learning, and demonstrate proficiencies? What are the student's responsibilities for learning?

3. *Sequenced:* Learning proceeds in a realistic sequence that builds on basic knowledge while supporting higher-level thinking. Assessment is used to monitor progress and strengthen learning outcomes.

   Questions to Consider: Do students know their starting point for learning? Can they explain how learning progresses and how they can continuously show progress?

4. *Differentiated:* The emphasis is on continuous progress toward goals. Students have multiple and varied ways to learn and display mastery throughout the taxonomies. Learning opportunities incorporate choice and assessments rely on flexible measures.

   Questions to Consider: Do all students have reasonable and equitable ways to show their learning? Are supports, interventions, and resources available for those who need it?

5. *Visible:* Clear and unambiguous assessment criteria and expectations support and engage learners in assessment. Students can explain their outcomes in relation to the scoring criteria.

   Questions to Consider: Do all constituents, from students to community and policymakers, view assessment as an essential process that supports student and school success?

Think about It

Individually and then with your team, rate each of the following on a 1-to-4 scale.

1 = This occurs consistently and effectively throughout our school/district.
2 = Most schools/teachers are at a satisfactory level on this indicator.
3 = To some extent this is apparent.
4 = There is minimal evidence of this taking place.

To what degree do our assessments

A. Support our district and school mission statement? What's the evidence?
B. Align with meaningful standards and learning targets? What's the evidence?
C. Demonstrate best practices in assessment? What's the evidence?
D. Reflect a balance from formative to summative assessments? What's the evidence?
E. Rely on multiple types of assessments to make decisions about teaching and learning? What's the evidence?
F. Measure higher and deeper learning? What's the evidence?
G. Include constructive feedback and opportunities for improvement in support of student success? What's the evidence?
H. Engage students in assessment and as assessors? What's the evidence?
I. Provide a balance of quantitative and qualitative information on student learning? What's the evidence?
J. Get used by teachers to adjust their teaching? What's the evidence?
K. Emphasize student growth over final scores? What's the evidence?

1. What elements of an assessment system are currently in place? Consider coherence, methodology, rigor, clarity, accountability, responsiveness, and transparency.
2. What steps will you take to construct a more responsive assessment system?
3. What fundamentals of a balanced assessment system are currently in place? Consider elements such as alignment with mission, purposeful methodology, comprehensiveness, clarity, accountability, responsiveness, transparency, and consistency.

ASSESSMENT READY LESSON DESIGN

Lesson plans come from numerous sources. They may be designed by teachers, included with the curriculum, or externally mandated. Whatever the source, there are feasible ways to strengthen their instructional and assessment friendliness. The assessment-readiness lesson plan in table 3.1 includes examples that can be adapted to your setting and purposes.

Table 3.1. Assessment-Readiness Lesson Design

Concept	In Practice
STANDARD ELA: Reading informational texts Learning Intention: Recognize and explain or show how ideas and information are related.	Science: Animal habitats or weather patterns Social Studies: Colonization or conflicts ELA: Similarities between source materials Art: Comparisons of works of art
Step 1: READINESS Assess prior learning and monitor readiness for learning.	Preassessment can include a KWL (we Know, Want to Know, and how we can Learn it) or a pretest similar to the posttest. With eyes closed, students display hand signals to indicate what they know and/or how they can do it successfully, somewhat, or not so much.
Step 2: READINESS Deconstruct standards into learning intentions that are understandable, assessable, and actionable.	What do your standards mean to the student? Use Post-it Notes (paper or electronic) for students to explain the meaning of the local learning intentions.
Step 3: READINESS Learning opportunities and actions support the standards and intentions.	This is specific to your classroom and may range from teacher-directed learning, to project-based, student demonstrations of learning, or teaching others. Formative assessments continuously monitor learning in relation to goals.
Step 4: TRANSITIONING TO OWNERSHIP Engage students in assessment. Students track the learning process and outcomes.	Students increasingly rely on their own selection of resources and have a growing choice in displaying their learning. They may rely on more formal assessments such as tracking progress on each of the learning intentions. Or, less formally, reflect and explain: "I used to think, but now I know."
Step 5: TRANSITIONING TO AGENCY Students take responsibility for planning and monitoring learning. Evidence of progress is made visible. Formative assessments lead to or increase/foster/augment readiness and adjustment of reflection modifications.	As students become more proficient at assessing their own learning, the responsibility transfers to them. With decreasing reliance on teachers for evaluating the learning, they become more proficient and comfortable in assessing their own learning. Teach what you learned to a Martian or give an elevator pitch for peers to assess and give feedback in relation to learning intentions.

Think about It

As you reflect on ways to adapt these ideas to your setting, here are a few questions:

1. What resources can you use to learn more and build your skills? Think about what you can read, watch, ask, or observe.
2. What are some low-risk ways you can practice or try out your emerging ideas and skills?
3. What types of evidence will you be looking for to confirm that you have learned what you planned on learning?
4. What results and outcomes do you want/anticipate for you and your students?

Part II

Chapter Four

Assessment-Ready Learners

Figure 4.1. Success starts with the first step

Take the first step, even when you don't see the whole staircase.

—Martin Luther King Jr.

Assessment-ready learners

1. recognize the life-skills, mindsets, personal attributes, and academic foundations of participatory assessment;
2. rely on big-picture standards that are deconstructed, evident, explicit, and tangible;
3. reflect and take action on the underlying routines and practices that support assessment readiness.

All teachers want to help their students succeed in school and each student brings unique goals for his or her own life. But what is it that leads some people to educational achievement and a successful path through life while other lives are more difficult to navigate? To ensure student success for all, educators must consider those personality traits, socioeconomic factors, role models, and life experiences that shape each student's achievement. Certain circumstances such as poverty, have a significant effect on life's outcomes, yet some students who are raised in poverty thrive. And, others raised with every advantage do not.

Life is a process of assessment from Pre-K readiness, to college acceptance, and job performance. Yet, it's not always easy to quantify educational achievement. For some, academic success means high scores on basic skills and for others problem solving and design thinking. Taking a broader view, assessment includes all the actions and steps taken throughout teaching and learning that provide evidence of outcomes of learning. In turn, these demonstrations of learning inform modifications to teaching and fine-tuning of learning. However, as Lorrie Shepard (2000, 4) reminds, "Assessment and instruction are often conceived as curiously separate in both time and purpose." However, they shouldn't be.

Assessment readiness can be viewed through academic and personal lenses. Robust academic foundations in all subjects support continuous learning. Readiness is also influenced by noncognitive factors such as resilience, persistence, and self-regulation. It also requires the ability to put things in perspective and merge diverse ideas in order to solve unique problems. In varied settings it can mean understanding subtraction, or practicing balance before peddling a bicycle, or monitoring emerging emotions during learning.

Assessment readiness varies between individuals. One person may have attuned spatial awareness that allows him or her to hike through the woods without a map. Another may need only a compass, and a third requires a personal trail guide and step-by-step route guidance. These understandings are important in preparing all learners to be assessment ready. It means that there is not one definition that applies to all learners at each stage of development. It does mean that there are sequences and strategies that can sustain all learners on their path to personal success.

FOUNDATIONS OF READINESS

This chapter focuses on the practicalities of preparing students for assessment. Brilliant lesson plans delivered by high-quality teachers may be a good starting point but may not be enough to ensure that all students have opportunities to climb their learning ladder and strive to achieve their goals. The qualities described here are the essential foundations for assessment-ready learners.

Life-Readiness: Few people are fully prepared for every challenge or curve-ball life throws at them. To add to the confusion, advice for living in the world includes many opposing views. For example, "Don't sweat the small stuff" versus "There is no small stuff" or "Don't wait for tomorrow" versus "It'll be better tomorrow." Students need more than platitudes to manage the fast pace, rapid changes, and obstacles on their path. Life readiness means that students can take a wide-angle view of life and have the knowledge and skills to make informed decisions and resolve problems.

Academic Foundations: Students' experiences in school can vary widely. Some are academically ready to begin each school year and others struggle with making routine progress. Academic achievement is more than content knowledge. It also requires knowing how to apply learning, adjust learning strategies, and continually adapt to new ideas.

Intrapersonal Skills: Efficacious assessors rely on an accurate and well-defined sense of self. They value personal strengths such as metacognition and problem solving and also recognize limitations such as impulsiveness. In general, these skills are less biologically based and more experientially influenced. In relation to assessment, students can learn the importance of mindset and rely on acquired strategies to strengthen intrinsic motivation.

Engagement: Being present and being involved in learning is essential. In a world of constant distractions, some suggest that the typical ten-minute attention span is shrinking. But being deeply involved in an activity is associated with positive academic outcomes. Engagement is a partnership between teachers who understand how to purposefully plan relevant lessons and students who are willing to give it a try.

Focus on Improvement: No one likes to make mistakes. Most people find it upsetting. But for some students, it means failure, and that becomes immobilizing. Rather, emphasize that growth is more valuable than final scores. Show students how to get help in making corrections; acknowledge evidence of their improvement; identify and celebrate small steps; and, most importantly, recognize how the correction of mistakes leads to improved learning outcomes.

Personal Responsibility: Ownership of assessment is an outcome of ownership of learning. Feasible priorities and attainable goals are a starting point. Owning responsibility requires a commitment to taking the steps that lead to your goals. Personal responsibility is built on insight, reflection, and prior success. It is typical for younger students to deflect blame. But with experience, learners begin to recognize the value of accepting responsibility for their thoughts, personal conduct, and actions.

Building on these foundations, teachers can take a look at the groundwork of success for all students. This means thinking about the beliefs, habits, and underpinnings that prepare and support students as insightful self-assessors.

Think about It: What Are Your Priorities?

> **REFLECTION ON STUDENT READINESS FOR SELF-ASSESSMENT**
>
> Checklists are one way to break down complex learning tasks. This list includes indicators of student readiness to become self-assessors. Prioritize your top two or three assessment-ready indicators. Feel free to include additional ones that may be important in your setting. With your learning team discuss similarities and differences. Identify the group's highest priorities.
>
> My/Our priorities are for developing assessment-ready learners who have these qualities:
>
> _____ 1. Understand how big-picture standards plot the course for learning
> _____ 2. Recognize how standards can be deconstructed into steps and sequences
> _____ 3. Are willing to be responsible decisions-makers
> _____ 4. Have the skills and mindsets necessary to persist in learning
> _____ 5. Believe/understand that learning improves through dedication and hard work
> _____ 6. Accept missteps in learning as opportunities for improvement and learn from experience
> _____ 7. Display curiosity about learning
> _____ 8. Take responsibility for their learning outcomes
> _____ 9. Articulate their own feelings and thoughts during the learning and assessment process
> _____ 10. Are willing to work with others to improve learning outcomes for all

ASSESSMENT-READY MINDSETS AND SCHOOLS

Assessment-Ready Mindsets

Here are two essential elements to ensure that students' brains are ready for assessment:

1. Reducing Assessment Stress: In a split second, a student may find herself ready to fight or prepared to flee. This normal human stress reaction of fight or flight is activated by a need for survival. The limbic system, located deep within the brain, is the primary emotional response center. When the amygdala, a small gland within, senses stress, it sends a signal to the hypothalamus that activates the nervous system to fight or flee. It is also activated when a student anticipates failure or senses hostility from others. Low-stress assessments that are aligned with the learning purpose and process are indispensable. Also, scaffolded and sequenced assessments can further readiness and sustain learning.

2. Brain-Friendly Assessment: Learning is a dynamic process. Synapses in the brain are firing and neurons are continuously making connections. Sitting passively and processing learning through a single modality such as listening or completing worksheets is not as effective as participatory learning. Brain-friendly assessments actively involve learners. This may include collaborative actions such as think-pair-share, generating other possible solutions or outcomes, summarizing learning visually, or transferring learning to another situation.

Assessment readiness is the foundation for engagement. It leads to students who are empowered as assessors. Assessment not only measures and reports learning but more importantly supports learners.

Assessment-Ready Schools

Below are three essential elements to ensure that schools are ready for high-quality student assessment.

1. Safety: Safety in assessment comes when students have a clear understanding of the learning intentions and also the opportunity to personalize and adjust them in ways that support their successes. This may mean deconstructing large-scale standards into actionable and measurable interim steps. For example, Stella says, "Compare two decimals by reasoning about their size (i.e., CCSS Math 4.NF.C.7)" means "I can read and understand decimals and put them in descending order."

2. Climate and Culture: A positive, affirming, and accepting school climate and culture is also important for assessment readiness. Students need to feel that their school is safe, not just physically, but also socially and emotionally. In relation to assessment, this requires a climate of respect for all, acceptance of mistakes as opportunities for learning, and encouragement of self-efficacy.

3. Preparing Students: Assessment-ready schools take all the needed steps to prepare all students for assessment. It is expected that they help all children not only achieve their highest level of proficiency but also help them achieve grade-level standards across the curriculum. In theory, this is an admirable goal. In reality, it is more important and less stressful to the learner for schools to prepare them to achieve their highest potential for achievement.

What is most important in assessment-ready schools is that all students have access to high expectations coupled with appropriate resources that support achievable levels of competency. Whether you call it standards, competency, proficiency, or mastery based, what is important is that all learners are ready for assessment. This begins with the S in SOAR, which represents Students, Standards, and Strategies. As they begin their journey,

- assessment-ready *students* understand how big-picture *standards* lead to local and personal learning intentions, and
- they begin to visualize and plan the *strategies, sequences,* and *structures* for learning and assessing.

Understanding Standards: Deconstructed and Attuned for Students and Settings

Students can best understand the learning goals, intents, processes, and outcomes when big-picture standards are deconstructed into their teachable, learnable, and assessable elements. Many, if not most, standards are simply too big. The examples below require additional clarification to make them easier to understand, take action, and become achievable for all learners.

CCSS.ELA-Literacy.L.2.3: Determine the meaning of words and phrases as they are used in a text (at grade-level complexity). For example, what is the meaning of "refuse" in line 5? This requires:

- mastery of grade-level vocabulary;
- ability to infer meaning from words and text;
- relying on sentence context for clues to the meaning;
- recognizing the root word in determining meaning.

CCSS.ELA-Literacy.RI.7.8: Trace and evaluate the argument and specific claims in a text, assessing whether the reasoning is sound and the evidence is relevant and sufficient to support the claims. This requires:

- defining and differentiating the meanings of argument and claim: *This is achievable.*
- explaining the author's claim(s) in your own words: *Students may need help.*
- distinguishing between claims that are supported and unsupported: *Mastery of new concepts, such as separating fact from fiction, requires focused instruction.*

- evaluating the argument and the claims: *Making judgments about its worth requires higher-level thinking.*

CCSS.Math.Content.1.OA.A.1: Use addition and subtraction within 20 to solve word problems involving situations of adding to, taking from, putting together, taking apart, and comparing, with unknowns in all positions (e.g., by using objects, drawings, and equations with a symbol for the unknown number to represent the problem). This requires:

- understanding the vocabulary of addition and subtraction: *May be more difficult for English-language learners.*
- representing addition and subtraction with objects, illustrations, words, or equations: *Objects and illustrations may be feasible. Words and equations will likely require support.*

This is a good place to pause and consider what this looks and feels like in your setting. To personalize your learning, begin by selecting a standard from your grade level or content area. Deconstruct it into the essential knowledge and skills that students are expected to master. Then translate those into student-friendly, understandable, and actionable learning goals, processes, and outcomes. Below are some examples of large-scale standards.

- CCSS.ELA-Literacy.RI.7.9: Analyze how two or more authors writing about the same topic shape their presentations of key information by emphasizing different evidence or advancing different interpretations of facts.
- CCSS.ELA-Literacy.W.2.1: Write opinion pieces in which they introduce the topic or book they are writing about, state an opinion, supply reasons that support the opinion, use linking words (e.g., *because, and, also*) to connect opinion and reasons, and provide a concluding statement or section.
- CCSS.Math.Content.6.SP.B.5.C: Giving quantitative measures of center (median and/or mean) and variability (interquartile range and/or mean absolute deviation), as well as describing any overall pattern and any striking deviations from the overall pattern with reference to the context in which the data were gathered.

Whether it be the life cycle of bees or the causes and strategies of war, students need help in making sense of learning objectives and developing strategies and sequences for learning through the taxonomies.

Recognizing Success Criteria: Deconstructed, Understandable, Actionable

Students can vary in how they write their success criteria. At one end of the quality spectrum is the student who says, "I will write a mystery story. I will use adjectives to make it spooky." Stretching beyond these foundations, another student may write, "I will write and edit a well-sequenced story that includes a coherent beginning, middle, and conclusion, utilize proper English conventions, and incorporate evidence of achieving the learning intention."

In science, a student-designed science experiment includes a definition of the problem; purposeful questions; a clear description of the process; a review of the current state of knowledge; and the hypotheses, procedures, and results. The scoring rubric includes criteria for evaluating the statement of the problem, procedures followed, and the accuracy of the interpretation of data. Table 4.1 shows an example of a student self-assessment rubric for assessing readiness skills and alignment with the learning intention. You will find more discussion of rubrics and their design in upcoming chapters.

Table 4.1. Reflection on Student Readiness for Assessment

Rubric for My Project

Points: 5	3	1	My Ratings & Insights
I checked my work for accuracy.	It looks like it's accurate.	There may be some errors.	
I included all the required parts.	Most of the parts are included.	I think I missed some parts.	
I was self-reliant and asked for help as needed.	It's mostly my work, but I got some help.	I needed some extra support and encouragement.	
My work shows effort.	I tried hard, but maybe not my best.	I put it together hurriedly.	
My work is complete.	My assignment is mostly done.	I skipped steps 3 and 5.	

Comments and Reflections:

FORTIFYING ASSESSMENT READINESS

Assessment readiness requires more than academic qualities. Earlier in this chapter, you were able to consider students' readiness elements, such as academic foundations and motivation to learn. The next two reflections ask the teacher and their students to reflect on additional physical readiness, self-awareness, learning routines, preferences, and practices that support assessment readiness. This is adaptable for your community and school as some settings rely on pertinent social skills and others more self-awareness and metacognitive skills.

Student Reflections: Preparing Learners for Assessment

Table 4.2. I Am Prepared to Learn and Self-Assess

Review the statements below and rate your readiness to move forward with your own learning. In the comments section, include actions that will ensure you will be effective in your learning when completing your classwork, and reflecting on and assessing your learning.

I am feeling	Overwhelmed	Tired	Ready	Topnotch
	Never	Rarely	Sometimes	Mostly
I get eight hours of sleep in my own bed.				
I eat a nutritious breakfast.				
I bring my homework and supplies to school.				
My assignments are complete and ready to turn in.				
I am optimistic about my learning and achievement.				
I am aware of and can use my strengths to sustain my achievement.				
I have strategies for self-assessing my accomplishments.				
When I get stressed, I can use one of my stress-management strategies.				

Comments and recommendations:

Elaborate on your ratings and propose changes you can make. Talk these over with your family and teachers.

Examples:
- Marinda says, "I love and will practice the head-to-toe relaxation exercise we did in class."
- Carrera says, "I'll work harder at reminding myself of successes rather than dwelling mostly on my failures."

MY PERSONAL ASSESSMENT-READINESS SCALE

Reflect on these contrasting views on your style of learning. Note where you are on each of the connecting lines.

1. I learn best when
I read about it...I watch about it

2. I learn best when
I work alone..I work with a group

3. When I have to publically share my learning
I'm really scared...I can't wait to be heard

4. When a problem is hard,
I tend to keep at it...……….I give up

5. My experiences in school have been
Successful..……….Disappointing

6. My general approach to life and learning is
Intense and forceful...…..Easygoing

7. When it comes to compromising, I
Find it difficult..Believe we can work it out

8. Most of the time I
Can learn independently...Need help to learn

9. For the most part
I get along well with others............................People get on my nerves

10. In the classroom, when it's time to learn, I prefer to
Be given specific directions.......................Figure things out on my own

11. When it comes to school
I really don't care about much.....................I'm curious about learning

    Begin by choosing a few of the indicators that you would like to move the meter on. For each one you select, reflect on your current position and suggest steps that you can take to move it.

    EXAMPLE for #5: Ainsley says, "I can do better if I remember to bring my stuff to school. To help me remember, I will put a checklist at my exit door and check off each step before I leave. I'll try a checklist app or a dry-erase board and see which works better. Then I'll track my improvement and celebrate when I see success."

READY TO TRANSFER RESPONSIBILITY FOR ASSESSMENT

There are numerous models for transferring responsibility for learning from teacher to student such as the "gradual release of responsibility" and "I do, we do, you do." Generally, these involve a teacher modeling the learning along with guided practice, followed by students' independent practice. There are also ways to transfer responsibility for assessment. These ideas will be elaborated and modeled throughout this book, but here are a few to begin to think about:

- *Questioning:* What levels of the taxonomy are most of your current classroom assignments and assessment questions? Wherever you are now, consider including stretching assessments into higher levels. For example, if questions are mostly recall and understanding, ask students how they can use the learning. Have them question two contrasting news reports on the same event or ask questions about the steps the sales agent took in calculating his car financing rates.
- *Making Connections:* Aldous often complains that he doesn't see why he has to learn about things that have no relevance to real life. Rather than justifying learning, ask students to submit responses to the question, "Why do I have to learn this?" Acknowledge the most accurate, creative, or illogical responses. Jacy's response, "For my own benefit!" is less reasoned and informative than Jaquille who says, "I understand the nutrition guidelines and know I am too picky about what I eat. Trying something prepared differently may make it tastier, so I might try it."
- *Fact or Fiction:* Provide students with a variety of news headlines. These might include "Discovered: A gene that makes you need less sleep"; "Math classes canceled due to changes in global numbering systems"; and "To be fair, all countries will be given nuclear weapons." Then have students write questions that they want to be answered about the headline. This leads to the development of research skills, sorting fact from fiction, and relying on defensible ideas rather than opinions. Ultimately, these news headlines will lead students to an analysis and evaluation of social media, fake news, or scientific claims.
- *Think Alouds:* As a closure or preparation for assessment, ask students to write the review questions. Then the teacher verbalizes his thinking as he answers and reflects on one of the questions. Mr. Matissa thinks out loud to "What evidence is there of life on other planets?" In another class, students respond to Ms. Armon's math question, "If one-third of the class wants pepperoni pizza, and each pizza serves four people, how many pepperoni pizzas should I order?" In this way, students begin to understand that

selected choice questions offer little opportunity to explain your answers. In response to this teacher's modeling, offer opportunities for students to explain their answers on their test questions.
- *Progressive Assessments:* These assessments are sequenced through the taxonomy. As students display learning from content knowledge to applications of learning, they are routinely reminded of the learning intentions in relation to what they learned in class. This sequence also develops self-confidence and willingness to continue to higher levels of learning. If we teach toward more complex learning outcomes, assessments should also move through a similar sequence. No rocket scientist was ever expected in second grade to build a rocket to carry a Tesla to Mars or a dinosaur's DNA to the Andromeda Galaxy.

Table 4.3. Applying SOAR to Student Readiness

Acronym	Indicates/ Represents	In Practice
S	Student Standards Strategies	From the start, students understand how big-picture *standards* lead to local and personal learning intentions. They begin to visualize and plan the *strategies, sequences, and structures* for learning/assessing.
O	Ownership Organization Onus	Students take *ownership* and *onus* (responsibility) for designing, *organizing*, and personalizing learning and assessment. With support, they develop plans that are well-defined, feasible, and actionable.
A	Agency Accountability Achievement	As students become *agents* of learning and assessment, their interest and attentiveness increases. Perseverance and *accountability* lead to higher levels of *achievement* and insightful *self-assessment*.
R	Results Review Respond	Results of student ownership and agency are evident in learning *results* and mindful *reflections*. Students are increasingly willing to *review, reassess,* and responsively modify outcomes with an emphasis on improvement.

Once students are academically ready, their basic needs are met, and they feel secure in their classroom, they are prepared to move forward with their readiness for assessment. Inclusion and belonging are the next step on Maslow's (1943) hierarchy toward success. Standardized tests may not typically support these mindsets for struggling learners, but here are classroom techniques that do:

- Assessments should engage learners and give them voice such as adding annotations to their responses and asking lingering questions within the assessments.
- Formative assessments include frequent check-ins for understanding as well as feedback that provides clarification on misunderstandings and guidance on next steps.
- Developing students as peer coaches can provide useful structured feedback with prompts such as: "What you said about ___ is very clear, but I'm still confused on ___" or "I see you included ___ but have you also thought about ___?"

As students mature, they develop clearer ideas about who they are and how they think. They also begin to identify their strengths and recognize personal struggles. This development of self-awareness and self-esteem can be fostered by assessments that encourage and guide students in monitoring their own learning. As students become reflective and flexible assessors, they can begin to personalize learning outcomes. For example, when given a choice to document their learning, Wei decides to make an instructive video, while Fiona illustrates a user's guide to learning.

One day, Max said to his teacher, "I want to try something new for my project, but don't want to be penalized for creativity, since it's the first time I'm using Piktochart, an infographic maker." After a brief conversation, Max and his teacher mutually agreed to count the content ratings of the rubric at 90 percent and the design ratings at 10 percent. With the pressure off, Max is inspired to try something new.

In the classroom, numerous elements of assessment have been shown to increase student success. These include:

- Clarity of purpose
- Relevance to the learner
- Engagement
- Authentic experiences
- Personal reflection
- Informative feedback
- Reliance on consistent assessment

Assessment Readiness Matters

If we can't see directly into students' brains, then seeing the outcomes (cognitive and emotional) of their learning is what we can rely on. Students' internal voices such as "I don't care" or "I'll try harder" are made visible through behaviors and products of learning. Sometimes, "Give it some more effort" or "I know you can do better" is often the default response. To boost success, it is more informative to ask, "What do you want to learn about this topic?" or "What support and resources do you most need?" You can clarify a student's need for guidance by asking, "What is frustrating you right now?" or "How can I help you with your next step?"

Developing a constructive right outlook is the first step in helping students assess their own learning. Think about your students and their assessment readiness. What comments do you hear from the students that they are assessment ready? What mindset is evident? What actions do you see? What can you do to prepare all students to be assessment-ready learners?

Think about It: Are Your Students Assessment Ready?

EVALUATING ASSESSMENT-READY LEARNERS

With your learning team, rate each of these expectations and requirements for assessment-ready learners. Provide commendations and recommendations on each to further your work.

5 = Exceeds Requirements 3 = Meets Expectations 1 = Needs improvement

_____ 1. From the start, students know what they will be learning and how their learning will be assessed. Examples include the various types of content questions, how learning will be measured, and what students will be expected to do to complete the test.

_____ 2. We can confirm that the assessments align with the content and process of learning.

_____ 3. Assessment strategies stretch learners beyond a bubble sheet of correct answers. They consist of multiple strategies from selected choices to products, performances, and artistic creations.

_____ 4. Assessments include multiple levels of thinking, from knowledge to synthesis and production of new ideas.

_____ 5. Assessment is instructionally informative and supportive. Results can be used to guide and strengthen teaching and learning.

_____ 6. The instrument is sensitive to and incorporates students' real-world experiences.

_____ 7. It offers choice in assessment. Students have individualized opportunities to show what they know and can do.

_____ 8. Assessment strategies engage students through analysis of a situation; problem solving; recognizing patterns; making decisions; or generating examples, models, and products.

_____ 9. Learning outcomes are evident. Growth is emphasized over final scores.

_____ 10. Consider the motivational/discouragement factor of the assessment. Is the language accessible for all learners? Are students confident about their skills and knowledge? Are they prepared for the test?

CASE STUDY

At the beginning of the school year, the grade-level teaching team at the Community School was discussing their students' lack of interest in completing assignments and assessments. Basically, their kids were showing up but weren't prepared for learning. They noted an improvement in attendance as a result of the previous year's efforts in partnering with parents and celebrating students' success.

This year was off to a good start attendance-wise, but after a few weeks, the teachers noticed that while the students were present, they weren't ready to fully participate in the learning and assessment. They observed that using entrance slips to check for incoming understanding was grabbing students' interest. Also, providing opportunities for students to share what they know, compare it to others, and fact-check, was also engaging. Students said they felt respected when asked to make connections between their learning and their life experiences. These changes were having positive effects on participation.

The teachers felt ready to take it to the next level. They began by developing a series of self-reflections for themselves:

- What are the pre-assessments telling us about students' knowledge, skills, and interests?
- How can we use this information to adapt instructional plans and guide teaching?
- How can we do this while still adhering to our school's instructional expectations and requirements?

- Based on incoming proficiencies, how can we ensure that each learner is ready to learn and prepared to be assessed? How can we know when the whole class is ready to move forward with the learning intentions?

REFLECTION

- What would you add to these questions?
- What is your analysis of their steps in developing student readiness for learning and assessment?
- If you feel that your team has already considered these questions, what would you add to them?

FINAL NOTE

Educators understand that the criteria for readiness that were described at the beginning of this chapter are shaped by both internal and external factors that may include:

1. Recognizing the life skills, mindsets, personal attributes, and academic foundations of participatory assessment
2. Relying on big picture standards that are deconstructed, evident, explicit, and tangible
3. Teachers and students reflecting and taking action on the underlying routines and practices that support assessment readiness

Numerous studies have described the development of and influences on social and emotional skills (i.e., noncognitive). McCormick, Cappella, and O'Connor (2015) summarize their findings as well as the results of other studies that confirm the connection. As such, although the book's focus is on developing assessment-ready learners, it is also essential to weave in the numerous nonacademic factors that influence student assessment outcomes.

Chapter Five

Engaging Students in Assessment

Figure 5.1. Engage me and I learn

Tell me and I forget. Teach me and I remember. Involve me and I learn.

—Benjamin Franklin

Engaged learners

1. find motivation and personal meaning in learning and assessing;
2. rely on verified practices and routines for practical and participatory assessment;
3. display indicators of engagement including interest, purpose, and resolve.

Engagement is at the heart of motivation. This applies to preschoolers playing tee ball as well as to adults in the workplace and teachers in the classroom. When third grader Torrance says he is not interested in playing ball but wants to ride a horse, his father says they can't afford riding so he has to play ball. As a result, he's disengaged and wanders around the outfield without purpose.

After reading about "boring" poets and traditional poetry forms in English class, Keenan hastily decides he loathes poetry, so he writes an original rap to describe DNA. When his teacher returns his "poem," the note says that it doesn't align with the school's writing standards for supporting claims with evidence. Here's a small segment of Keenan's poem in which he explains deoxyribonucleic acid, its structure, and purpose.

> *Listen to a story that I'm going to tell.*
> *How DNA is found inside all your cells.*
> *In your hair, blood, skin, and lungs as well;*
> *Even got some DNA to help me smell.*
> *My DNA is not for your replication.*
> *Use your own nucleic a' for your mutation.*
> *Keenan wants no part of your creation.*
> *I need my DNA for life's duration.*

Fortunately for Keenan, his uncle is a teacher and explains there are two writing standards that are part of supporting claims with evidence. These include "developing the topic with relevant facts" and "providing a concluding statement that follows the argument." He also clarifies that poetry can take many forms.

While the standards don't specifically mention poetry, Keenan's teacher is willing to listen as he reasons that writing is about communicating; and his rap clearly communicates some principles of DNA. As a result of his teacher's aha moment, there are two positive outcomes: higher engagement for Keenan and a deeper understanding of diverse perspectives on writing by the teacher. Additionally, Keenan uses the assignment to learn about how DNA is collected and whether organ transplants can change a person's DNA.

Kennan's third-grade sister, Keanna, gets so excited about his rap, that she asks her teacher if she can write one. The goal and intention is to prepare a summary of their unit on animal adaptations. In it, she is expected to explain the key ideas with evidence. With her brother's help she writes:

> *They say penguins and gulls are alike because*
> *Both have feathers and bones from past history.*
> *[The teacher suggests* antiquity, *so she looks it up and changes her rap.]*
> *Yet, one soars through air, the other through water.*
> *Adaptation means adjusting to some type of change.*
> *Maybe I'll grow feathers when the climate's rearranged.*

Both of their teachers develop scoring rubrics based on the district's criteria: clarity of information, organization, use of evidence, focus on topic, and accuracy. They decide to add their own indicators for reflection and creativity. At the dinner table, both students are enthusiastic about this personalization of learning and talk about rewriting their work in response to the feedback they received.

ENGAGEMENT AS MOTIVATION

When students aren't performing up to expectations, it is typical to start by assessing their academic skills. When the causes aren't academic, then inattention, mental health, or problems at home are explored. Sometimes, it's just plain boredom with the repetitiveness or irrelevance of the classroom that leads to a student's lack of interest and disengagement. However, there are numerous substantiated reasons to make student engagement a priority. An essential component of engagement is that it changes a school and classroom from a culture of testing and measuring learners to a culture of involvement in learning and improvement in outcomes that includes the concepts outlined below.

Personalizing learning is motivational:

- *Allows for differentiated techniques and methods:* There are multiple pathways for achieving goals. Students may decide to display their achievement of the learning criteria in an infographic, model, video, or medium of interest to them.
- *Builds trust:* Social and emotional skills are the mainstay of learning. Relationships and mutual respect are developed when students feel their ideas are valued.
- *Compels various types of learning opportunities:* In an engaged classroom, options for learning are essential. For students who may not have the highest writing scores, relying on images or recordings to show their learning can be just as effective as writing them.
- *Recognizes the explicit learning expectations:* Students feel more confident when they understand how much and how deeply they are expected to master the learning standards and can see their relevance before starting their learning journey.

Involvement in learning is motivational:

- *Encourages effort:* When students feel that their classroom is a safe place to express their ideas, they are more willing to reach toward higher levels of learning. They know that mistakes are part of learning.

- *Supports intrinsic motivation:* A desire to learn is essential. When students are comfortable and interested, they are more apt to take ownership, set goals, and determine a course of action.
- *Boosts metacognition:* The use of prompts and questions such as "What would you do, and why?" or "What evidence do you have of progress?" helps students dig more deeply into their thinking.
- *Leads to ownership of learning:* Ultimately students become the owners and proprietors of assessment and take responsibility for their own learning outcomes.

Evidence of improvement is motivational:

- *Contributes to a growth mindset*: Students who understand the learning goals and processes develop a sense of responsibility for their outcomes. They recognize that practice leads to improvement.
- *Promotes growth:* As a result of feeling safe and supported, students are more willing to take on some learning risks and reasonably struggle as they know that this is a valuable pathway to success.
- *Provides balanced insights into learning:* Rather than compiling data from a small number of test results, students can define and exhibit their own learning outcomes. Thus, broadening the meaning of evidence of learning can include writing, artifacts, and creative expression.
- *Strengthens overall assessment:* Assessment is strengthened when it relies on consistent and clearly defined learning outcomes and evidence of learning.

Engagement matters for teachers too. Managing an ever-increasing workload and being expected to say yes to every request from students, parents, and administrators can be stressful. Engaging teachers in meaningful professional growth and providing time to collaborate, leads to higher morale, motivation, accountability, and reflection, all in support of student learning.

Mr. Marcus has been trying out different engagement strategies during the past few months. He finds that his students like games and puzzles. In one lesson, he handed out cards with part of a sequence and had students line up in the correct order. Another time he had students design a game board, such as Candyland, with questions on each card. Students traded their games and gave feedback on the questions to the designers. In the past he has also used pre-made Jeopardy templates. Rather than writing all the questions, he wants to turn over that responsibility to the students. He demonstrates how to write questions with one correct answer. Examples include:

- Article IV of the U.S. Constitution explains the procedure for admitting new ones of these to the union. _____?
- The number of years between 776 BC, when the Olympic games began, and 1896 AD when they were finally resumed. _____?
- In Poe's poem, the raven repeatedly says this word. _____?
- *The Little Mermaid* was based on a classic fairy tale written by him. _____?
- Another name for the white of an egg. _____?
- The correct spellings of filanthopist (a generous donor) and cercumfrance (the perimeter of a circle) are _____.

Mr. Marcus's unit test begins with grade-level selected choice questions. He also includes opportunities for students to display deeper understanding by adding "Why did the Olympic games not take place in 1940? What is the meaning of the word the raven repeats in the poem? Describe parts of the story of *The Little Mermaid* that Disney kept or changed." For the application and analysis section, he offers options such as graphic organizers and various charts. Other teachers in his school find that this process works for a range of topics and have begun to include these motivational ideas in their classrooms.

WHAT DOES IT MEAN TO BE ENGAGED?

The sights and sounds of student engagement include:

- Walking into an engaged classroom, a visitor might be met with silence or raucousness. Students might be so enrapt in a teacher's science demonstration that they may not even notice someone walking in. Perhaps it is a lesson on surface tension and bubbles of all shapes are floating around the room.
- Alternatively, it can be a seemingly messy place as students experiment with different ingredients such as baking soda, baking powder, flour, vinegar, and oil and predict which mixture generates gas and will result in a bubbling cup of liquid or biscuit dough.

Flow theory was developed by Mihaly Csikszentmihalyi (2008) to explain those moments when people are so immersed and involved in an activity that they lose track of time and place and completely tune out any distractions. It may not be possible to generate this optimal focus in every student, but there are ways to make learning more personal and meaningful. John Spencer (2017) offers several ideas, including evidence of progress, appropriate scaffolds, intrinsic interest, practical learning, student choice, minimal interruptions, informative feedback, and opportunities for revision.

In the classroom, clear and actionable goals are a good start. Students then need to deconstruct standards and big-picture goals into their own individual learning aims and intentions. The level of challenge must be feasible for the students. If the goals are too easy, students will get bored and complete their assignment quickly. If the goals are too hard, students become discouraged leading to low-quality outcomes, or none at all.

Feedback is also an essential element of flow. This can be personal feedback through reflection on progress and outcomes, a self-scored rubric, and/or feedback from a peer or from a teacher. Students' statements of engagement include:

- "I understand the learning intentions and what I'm supposed to learn."
  "Now I know where and why we are heading there."
- "I know what I will do to reach them: read, highlight, and color code the categories."
  "I will start with this first step and see how it works out."
- "I can make progress. I'll take my time reading to see if I can understand the main ideas."
  "OK, the first step is done and I checked it against the criteria. I just need to adjust the tone."
- "This sounds interesting *and* possible. I have strong feelings on this topic and will try to curb my emotions."
  "OK, I'll give it another try. Now that I can see where I'm headed."

Engaging learners in assessment reduces the stress of learning something new. A little cortisol, the stress hormone, can whet the mind in anticipation of an assessment, but we don't want to raise it to a red-flag level. Finding the balance between attentiveness and anxiety differs from student to student. In any setting, there should be no assessment surprises. For example, asking students to apply learning in a somewhat different scenario than the one learned in class can raise anxiety, and students should be reassured that the process is the same. Stress from notetaking can be reduced by giving students empty outlines where they are picking out the appropriate word or phrase. Confidence in public speaking can be developed through the use of students' choice of a technology for electronic presentations.

Engagement is infrequently an element of traditional assessment, as tests are typically a solo activity. But when the roots of assessment are considered, the connections become clearer. Assessment comes from the Latin word *assidere*, which means "to sit beside as an assistant or advisor." These routine check-ins, informative feedback sessions, and opportunities for improvement are the engaging and relationship-based elements of assessment.

Sarine prefers predictability in assessment and Seiji sees himself as an assessment warrior. Sarine has learned the skills she needs to purposefully and diligently prepare for an upcoming test. She summarizes the main ideas and reviews what she was taught about its meaning and relevance and how it was used in class. She confidently digs into the example on the test. Seiji has a momentary panic attack before realizing that they did a similar problem in class and the flow of cortisol activates his brain, enabling him to do his best work.

SMART Model of Engagement

There are numerous goal-setting models. The SMART goal model shown here is a reliable and achievable strategy for students. It is an acronym for *Specific, Measurable, Attainable, Relevant, and Time-Based*. The model is made relevant for all learners by adjusting the language levels. For example, "What are my specific goals?" is simplified to "This is what I will learn." "What actions and steps will I take?" translates to "My first step will be."

Personalization of goals makes them more relevant, authentic, and interesting to learners. It begins when students evaluate their incoming knowledge and skills in relation to learning purposes and intentions and, in due course, to assess their learning outcomes. Table 5.1 shows the steps in the process. In the next chapter, you'll see the process in action.

Table 5.1. Incorporating SOAR into "SMART" Goal Setting

Goal	Planning: Questions to Consider in Setting Goals	Outcomes, Evidence, and Reflections: In Student's Words
S SPECIFIC and STRATEGIC	What are my explicit goals? How well do visible learning intentions support and align with the goals? What are the success criteria? *Example of simpler wording*: What do I plan on learning? How well will my plans lead to the goal? How will I know when I am successful?	
M MEASURABLE and MOTIVATIONAL	How will I know how well I achieved each goal? What evidence of achievement do I need? What qualitative and quantitative data are required? *Simplified*: My pretest score was ___. I want to get ___ by the end of the unit.	

(continued)

Table 5.1. (continued)

Goal	Planning: Questions to Consider in Setting Goals	Outcomes, Evidence, and Reflections: In Student's Words
A	What do I want and need to know and do?	
ACTIONABLE and ACHIEVABLE	What actions and steps will I take? How realistic/feasible are these plans?	
R	How does this build on my prior learning and support future learning?	
RELEVANT and REALISTIC	How will I be able to use my learning in and beyond the classroom?	
T	What is a feasible timetable for completing my plan?	
TIME-BASED and TANGIBLE	How can I monitor and make certain that I will stick to the plan?	

Personalizing Goals through Student Voice

Table 5.2 illustrates how Davi, a second-grade student personalized his learning goals and process in each of his subject areas. These goals combine his understanding of what he needs to learn at his grade level as well as his specific interests. As appropriate, this may start with peer feedback. Then Davi meets with his teacher to discuss his progress and, in due course, with his parents at student-parent conferences. He continues to modify his goals for each cycle. What you see in this example are Davi's resulting edited words after receiving feedback and revising them.

Table 5.2. Sample Personalized Learning Goals

Name: Davi **Grade:** 2–3

Content Area Standards	Student's Personal Learning Goal	Assessment Plan
Language Arts: CCSS: A Lexile represents the complexity of the text and individual reading ability. (CCSS Appendix)	I will continue to read 300–500 Lexile-level books for twenty minutes each night at home. *My goal is to be reading 450 to 650 level by April.*	I will maintain a record of the Lexile levels of the books I am reading. With my teacher, I will make sure the numbers are getting bigger.
Math: CCSS.2.oa.a.1: Solve one- and two-step word problems: adding to and taking from.	I am learning how to write stories about people. I want to describe what my family looks like, how they act, and what they are thinking as compared to my family's ancestors. I will continue to do my math homework; I will also complete a word problem every day at home in my workbook. *My parents try to help, but I still need more help from my teacher.*	I'll show the teacher my work, and when I get stuck, she can help me figure out what I didn't understand and what to do next.
Social Studies: Examine and identify cultural differences within the community.	I am creating a family history book with pictures, drawings, and stories about my ancestors and how they lived compared to how my family lives today. I got pictures of my family and ancestors. *I have written a story about the farm that my mother's parents lived on when she was a little girl and put them together in my family history book.*	I'll ask my peers to use the success criteria for my sequence, design, neatness, and clarity and give me feedback on how well I am doing with my family history book.
Science: NGSS 2-LS2-1: Investigate water and sunlight to see what plants need to grow.	I am learning how to create a garden plan and determine how much water and sunlight plants need. I am sketching vegetable growth each week when I work in the garden. *I have a journal for my notes and sketches. The tomatoes did not blossom because it was too cold. The zucchini plants are growing zucchinis that are ten inches long. They like the foggy fall weather.*	I will note what worked and what didn't and make specific suggestions for the next growing season.
Nutrition and Physical Activity	I will walk around the block at my home twice each day after school. *I want to aim for three loops in the same time period.* I will eat a nutritious breakfast each day before school. I will be able to explain what is contained in a nutritious breakfast *and compare my food choices.*	I will use a fitness tracker to record my laps and speed and look for improvement. I'll focus on reduced-fat milk, whole grains, lean meats, and fruits.
Other: Arts	I will continue practicing how to draw animals by copying from a book. *I will watch a YouTube video each week that shows me how to draw a different animal. I will then get feedback on my art.*	I will put all my drawings in order and ask the teacher in what ways they have improved or could be better.

(continued)

Table 5.2. (continued)

Name: Davi **Grade:** 2–3

Content Area Standards	Student's Personal Learning Goal	Assessment Plan
Other: Spanish	I will practice talking to my family in Spanish for five minutes each day. I hope to listen to some online kids' language tutorials. I have started recording my new words.	At dinner, we talk about the food in Spanish and look up ones we don't know. I am illustrating my own Spanish food dictionary.
Behavior: Manage emotions	I will keep a star chart at home in managing my emotions when I am angry or frustrated. I am learning how to go to my room and calm down. I'll ask my friend about the deep breathing and mindset exercises he learned.	Wow, belly breathing really works to calm me down. Maybe I will learn yoga.

Table 5.3. SOAR Analysis of Davi's SMART Goals

Acronym	Indicates/ Represents	In Practice
S	Student Standards Strategies	With assistance, Davi translated the big-picture standards into kid-friendly and actionable personal goals. He explained his understanding of his learning intentions and identified feasible strategies for achieving them.
O	Ownership Organization Onus	Davi had choices in what he wanted to emphasize and focus on and to decide how he would do so. He chose strategies, planned his learning, and tracked progress and demonstrated evidence of taking responsibility for his learning. He knew when to ask for help from his teacher and peers.
A	Agency Appraisal Achievement	Davi relied on his own goals. He customized them and explained ways to achieve them in ways that made sense to him. This led to increased levels of motivation as shown by his enthusiasm. He collaborated with his teacher to turn his planned learning outcomes into trackers, checklists, and rubrics.
R	Results Review Respond	Davi continued to monitor and revise his goals, adjust his learning, and monitor ongoing improvement. He understood that progress was the key to success. Eventually, he will learn how to align his learning outcomes with the lesson's learning intentions.

Engaging Reluctant Learners

Everyone has times that they are focused on faraway thoughts or looming problems, and then snap back to the present, unaware of what's been going on in the here and now. Students too, may be sitting in your classrooms, eyes open and heads forward, while worrying about a family member who is ill or daydreaming about an upcoming trip.

There's a difference between being present and being engaged. For students who have social, emotional, or learning difficulties, learning how not to be noticed can be a priority. These students may get passed on to the next grade or level because they do not have behavioral problems, but are rather quiet and compliant learners. By the time they get to high school, they can be several grade levels behind.

On behalf of those quiet and compliant learners, it is even more important to check for understanding, as a camouflaged lack of comprehension can lead to disengagement. Other causes of low engagement are developmental difficulties, struggles with self-regulation, and social/emotional hurdles. Many strategies for engaging students in assessment, as well as giving students ownership and agency, are elaborated in each of the upcoming chapters. To begin, the box below summarizes key ideas as a checklist to reflect on ways to engage students as assessors.

Think about It

> **CHECKLIST FOR TEACHERS ON STUDENT ENGAGEMENT**
>
> Assess your current strategies for engaging students in learning and assessing by completing the checklist below. Be honest about your accuracy as it is intended to be a baseline of your practice. In due course it can be used to guide adjustments to your routines. Rate yourself on a 1 to 5 scale with 1 being never and 5 being always. You are encouraged to add personal annotations with each concept.
>
> _____ 1. Verify that students understand the learning intentions and can explain them in their own words.
>
> _____ 2. Routinely check for understanding during the learning process.
>
> _____ 3. Respond to evidence of understanding with feedback, questions, prompts, and such.
>
> _____ 4. Model, encourage, support, and reinforce growth mindsets.
>
> _____ 5. Acknowledge and recognize each student's strengths and skills.
>
> _____ 6. Rely on culturally relevant teaching and learning.
>
> _____ 7. Help learners appreciate that mistakes are opportunities for learning and improvement.
>
> _____ 8. Routinely embed assessment directly into learning.
>
> _____ 9. Align assessment with learning intentions. Ask students to show where they see connections.
>
> _____ 10. Include/Assess multiple levels of learning taxonomies from knowing to producing.
>
> _____ 11. Include opportunities for students to be actively involved by explaining a decision or creating something.
>
> _____ 12. Provide feedback that is focused and actionable.
>
> _____ 13. Incorporate opportunities to self-score and self-correct assessments.

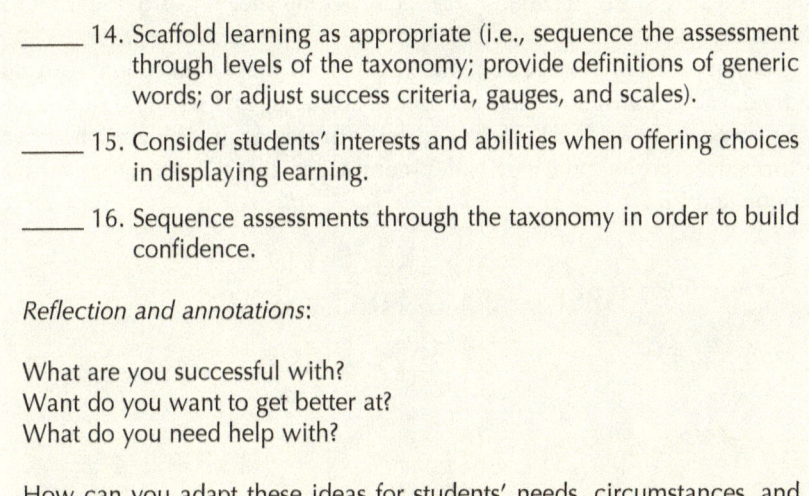

Individual attention spans are only a few minutes long and may be influenced by a student's interest, activity level, setting/location, or assigned group. Use strategies such as these to keep students engaged:

- Ask questions that require deeper and higher thinking and make connections to prior learning.
- Have students tell a partner what they just learned.
- Add movement to learning such as signals for agree/disagree, or sure/unsure.
- Ask students for periodic summaries and recaps: These can be submitted as individual check-in slips or collaborative summaries.

Frequent use of formative assessments can be fun as well as illuminating. Consider ways to use Twitter-length summative statements, spot the fake news article from a list of topical headlines, or illustrate a telescopic or microscopic view of a topic. Students can summarize and discuss various snowball activities where they ball up a paper, toss theirs, and grab another snowball to evaluate or answer.

They can be given one part of a sequence of events and work together to put them in the correct order. Students can watch examples and make their own educational video. The bottom line is that awareness and interest in learning are essential to engagement. Engagement is motivational. Whatever form engagement takes (e.g., intellectual, social, emotional, or physical), engaged learners are successful learners. Making meaning from learning is what's important.

The outcomes of engagement include more robust connections to prior learning, easier transfer of learning to new scenarios and settings, augmented responsiveness to feedback, increased self-efficacy as in analyzing their own performance results, and higher self-confidence to facilitate next steps in learning and life.

ASSESSMENTS THAT ENGAGE

Figure 5.2. Assessments that engage learners

> The curious mind is constantly alert and exploring, seeking material for thought. Eagerness for new experiences is found where wonder is found. Curiosity is the only sure guarantee of the acquisition of the primary facts upon which inference must base itself.
>
> —John Dewey (1910)

Mr. Kee likes to introduce a new lesson with a story that cultivates interest and attention, raises curiosity, or presents a mystery about the topic. Sometimes, as he uses an image or object to introduce a new concept, he also models a think aloud. One time, he showed a picture of an ending or outcome of an occurrence for students to ask questions about what it is and how it came to be. Another time he asked his middle schoolers about the Little Red Hen's process of decision making.

He then introduces the big-picture standard and explains three to four measurable learning outcomes for the lesson. Learning begins with an individual reflection or analysis of the topic. Students then work in small groups to gather additional information that may be needed to move forward with their learning, problem solving, or investigation. As they track their progress, they continually self-assess learning in relation to the learning intentions. They also take brief practice/formative assessments during learning.

Mr. Kee notes that some of the students clearly understand the process and outcomes, others need additional review, and several need focused tutoring. Before the grade-level common assessment, he groups students into those that would benefit from enrichment, those that need further review and reinforcement, and a choice of tutorials for other students. In doing so, he notices that his students are more engaged and show reduced stress responses.

Feet on the Ground, Eyes on the Sky: Focus on Purpose, Process, and Outcomes

On the one hand, rote learning takes the joy out of learning and can make learning tedious. On the other hand, electronic devices and games in the classroom can distract learners or simply be gamified rote learning. Maintaining a focus on learning outcomes, purposes, and processes can be challenging when the distractions are so attractive.

Sometimes diversions do work out for the best. Think about the unintended development of sticky notes by Spencer Silver as he was trying to invent a super-strong adhesive. Microwave ovens were invented when Percy Spencer, a radar scientist, noticed that the candy bars in his jacket pocket had melted. In the classroom, sometimes a distraction can benefit learning. And thinking about one problem can lead to solutions of others.

Stefan planned to learn more about radiation emanating from hand-held electronic devices and to make recommendations for reducing exposure to it. Pretty soon, his teacher discovered that Stefan was designing an EMF shielding device for his head. Stefan explained that he lived near overhead high-voltage power lines and wanted to protect his family. It was a dilemma for Ms. Wren to decide whether to let him continue on this alternative path. After their discussion, they agreed that Stefan could explain what he learned about EMFs and show how his device might prevent potential brain damage, whatever their source. He agreed that recording his steps and sequences in a graphic organizer would confirm that he developed an understanding of the basic concepts of radiation. They also decided that he would include a fact sheet comparing the fact and fiction of EMFs.

Stretching thinking to higher levels is not only for older students. Prompts and activities can be thoughtfully placed within most learning. Ask students to predict what a character will do next and brainstorm alternative decisions. Ask students to generate questions about a picture of early settlers or the Mars landing.

For many students, routine check-ins and intentional refocusing can make a big difference. It's a good idea to periodically check on the destination and even take a brief layover to reaffirm or revise goals and outcomes. In a student-engaged classroom, flexibility is essential. Take the time to refocus and realign learning by relying on reflective prompts such as "Am I still working toward my goal?" or "How can I get back on the path?" and "What if I found something else that interests me more?"

Check in on student understanding by asking them to "right the wrong" or correct answers to a math problem, capitalize letters, identify verbs versus adjectives, label organs in the body, or follow steps in a recipe or experiment. Examples include:

- At the start of the lab, the first thing Rosie did was *turn on the burner*.
- Which of these is not in the right place in the picture: the *heart, lungs, liver, stomach, or intestines?*
- Jetta wanted to smell the peach, so she used her *tongue*.
- The first prime number is *5*.
- World War II ended in *1943*.

Another strategy is to give students cards for something that happens in a sequence such as getting ready to go to school, or photosynthesis. This can be done with a partner or in groups. The following are examples of how assessment can become more engaging and meaningful:

- Make real-world connections. For example, what would happen if we had the Black Plague today?
- Incorporate fun and humor in learning: Have students make up riddles such as "Why shouldn't you tell secrets in the vegetable garden?" with an answer of "because the beanstalk."
- Review with student-generated responses to "Two Truths and a Lie" game.
- Ask a whole class to "spot the fake" headline and then ask students to write real and fake headlines to summarize their learning and for classmates to sort.
- Play student-designed games, such as Jeopardy or Trivia.
- Make it fun: shape playdough, play charades, write a song, create "Wanted" posters, make a map, or paint your "innards" on your "outards."

- Write a recipe that explains a character's traits for other students to guess (i.e., a dash of hot sauce and gardenia petals).
- Use technology such as Kahoot for quizzes, Linoit for student responses, or Quizlet to create study sets.

Responsive and Informative

What good is it if the team loses the game but never reviews the video of the plays? What will happen if the cake doesn't rise and the cook prepares it exactly the same way the next time? As learners' misunderstandings are identified, it is beneficial to correct errors while strengthening basic knowledge and skills. Formative assessment is about gathering data to inform teachers and students on progress. It serves as a guide to meaningful instructional responses and for students' modifications to learning.

The concept of formative assessment can be traced back to Michael Scriven (Tyler, Gagne, and Scriven, 1967), who used the terms *formative* and *summative* to indicate differences in both the goals for collecting evaluation information and how that information is then used. Since then, the research and evidence of the effectiveness of formative assessment continue to increase. As Libby Woodfin (Rugen, Woodfin, and Berger, 2014) states, "In our experience, what is more important than any particular formative assessment technique is a commitment to involving and investing students in the process."

As evidence of learning becomes visible, teachers also need to make decisions about actions to take in response to students' learning. These can focus on the achievement of the entire class or on individual students making progress at their own tempo. Consider the following when determining your plan of action:

Planning:

- Review and as necessary clarify learning intentions.
- Calibrate and balance levels of mastery for individual students based on their progress.
- Include exemplars of work at various levels of achievement for student review and self-assessment.

Teaching and learning:

- Decide how to group students for enrichment or reinforcement.
- Re-teach with an alternative instructional strategy, technology, or modality for learning.

- Adjust pacing of instruction.
- Modify the depth of learning.

Supporting student outcomes

- Chunk and reorganize material into groups and subsets.
- Furnish scaffolds to support students as they move up the learning ladder.
- Help students visualize learning with graphic organizers and digital resources.
- Provide focused and actionable feedback.
- Don't forget to take a break: stretch, get some fresh air, have fun, and share a snack.

THINK ABOUT IT

Summing up and synthesizing new ideas and practices require purpose, perseverance, and focus. As you move forward, engage students in learning and assessing. Here are two prompts to begin that process.

STEP 1: Consider these fundamental ideas about engaging students in learning. Each statement can be deconstructed into essential ideas, as they each include many elements of engagement. Think about what they mean to you. Discuss examples of what they currently look like in your setting. Also consider changes you want to make to current engagement practices including:

- The most effective feedback in relation to engagement is goal oriented, purposeful, practical, and focused on progress. Feedback has the potential to change a mindset from "I can't do this" to "I'll try it another way." Feedback is most effective when it emphasizes progress and growth.
- Engaging students in assessment means that their learning and assessment is focused on their goals, they know their current level and expected achievement, the emphasis is on progress and improvement, and the learning path is clear.

STEP 2: Rely on the SOAR model. As the ideas in this book emerged, were synthesized, and became organized, it became clear that opening the door to engagement starts with getting students' attention. Once the door begins to open, students can begin to engage more purposefully.

Think about ways you can make use of these ideas in the first step of SOAR as your starting point for student engagement.

At the beginning of this chapter, we explained that *engaged learners*

1. find motivation and meaning in learning and assessing;
2. rely on verified practices and routines for assessment;
3. display indicators of engagement such as interest, awareness of purpose, and increased resolve.

Think About: The SOAR Process

Table 5.4. Applying SOAR to Student Engagement

Acronym	Indicates/ Represents	In Practice
S	*Student* Standards Strategies	From the start, *students* understand how big-picture standards lead to local and personal learning intentions. They begin to visualize *strategies*, *sequences*, and *structures* for learning and assessing.
O	*Ownership* Organization Onus	Students take *ownership* and *onus* (responsibility) for designing, *organizing*, and personalizing learning and assessment. With support, they develop plans that are well-defined, feasible, and actionable.
A	*Agency* Appraisal Achievement	As students become *agents* of learning and assessment, their interest and attentiveness increase. Perseverance and *accountability* lead to higher levels of *achievement* and insightful *self-assessment*.
R	*Results* Review Respond	Results of student ownership and agency are evident in learning *results* and mindful *reflections*. Students are increasingly willing to *review*, *reassess*, and responsively modify outcomes with an emphasis on improvement.

Chapter Six

Developing Students as Owners of Assessment

Figure 6.1. When students become owners of their own assessment

Until the lion learns how to write, every story will glorify the hunter.

—African Proverb

Assessment-capable learners

1. recognize and appreciate the value of developing students as owners of assessment;
2. transfer the responsibility for assessment from teacher to learners;
3. transition from assessment readiness to assessment proprietorship.

There are times educators feel confident and dynamic and other times powerless and lethargic. It is important to focus on successes. It is also essential to reflect on times you felt powerless or drained of energy. Maybe it was when you were given compulsory study guides and schedules for upcoming mandatory tests, or perhaps experiencing initiative overload in your school. Powerlessness can turn to hopelessness when an individual sees no ending or feasible strategy for gaining control over the situation. Students, as well as adults, are happier, more energized, and productive at school or work when they feel they are accepted, involved, and have some degree of control.

In children's stories, characters are sometimes portrayed as powerless. Little Red Riding Hood was deceived by the wolf necessitating a rescue by the lumberjack. In a contrasting Russian version, Masha is able to entice the beast into safely returning her to her family. Evil stepmothers can render a hero or heroine powerless through fear, intimidation, or forfeiture. Self-esteem can undo their power. In relation to assessment, rather than mandatory test preparation, it is more effective to guide, support, and give students ownership of assessment.

What does happen when we give students power and control over their assessments? As Brookhart, Moss, and Long (2008) explain, "Paradoxically when teachers give students more control over their own assessment practices, more powerful learning happens" (52).

In addition to fairy tales and anecdotal evidence, the importance of assessment-capable learners is continuously emphasized throughout substantiated research and expert judgments. Consider these words on the value of empowering students as owners of assessment.

- *"If we want students to take charge of their learning, we cannot keep relegating them to a passive role in the assessment process"* (Frey, Fisher, and Hattie, 2018).
- *"The important question is not how assessment is defined but whether assessment information is used"* (Palomba and Banta, 1999).
- *"When anyone is trying to learn, feedback about the effort has three elements: redefinition of the desired goal, evidence about present position, and some understanding of a way to close the gap between the two"* (Black and Wiliam, 2010).
- *"Self-regulation of learning leads to increased student performance improvement"* (Wiliam, 2011).
- *"Students who engage in self-assessment are more likely to develop internal attributions, a feeling of empowerment, and a sense of autonomy"* (Dyer, 2015).

BENEFITS OF DEVELOPING ASSESSMENT-CAPABLE OWNERS OF ASSESSMENT

As students become increasingly engaged in assessment, opportunities for ownership also increase. Engagement builds trust, encourages effort, and advances a growth mindset. Empowerment leads to the development of students and teachers who self-regulate, collaborate, and recognize these benefits of assessment-capable learners.

Developing Thinking Skills

- *Supports multiple pathways for learning*
  - When students have a choice in both learning and displaying learning, they can rely on existing skills, such as comparing and generating ideas, and strengthen emerging skills, such as reliance on evidence.
- *Propels towards higher levels of achievement*
  - As students see that progress is equally, if not more, important than outcomes, they are willing to exert more effort.
- *Raises the quality of learning*
  - If students know that it's okay to struggle at first but also know that help is available, they are more likely to strive for higher levels of learning.

Developing Higher and Deeper Levels of Learning

- *Enhances practical and feasible problem-solving skills*
  - Problem solving and other types of higher-level thinking are typical routines of student engagement.
- *Encourages flexible and divergent thinking*
  - Students have opportunities to explore a topic in more depth, through multiple lenses, and measure their learning in personally relevant ways.
- *Extends insights into learning beyond the data*
  - Numbers and test scores can rank and compare students' past and current performance; however, varied comprehensive strategies offer deeper insights into the thinking behind the numbers.

Encouraging Self-Regulation and Self-Discipline

- *Facilitates students planning and goal setting*
  - When students know they have voice and choice in learning and also in displaying learning outcomes, they are more willing to formulate and follow their goals.

- *Strengthens self-directed learning*
  - Personal understanding of learning intentions, combined with a focus on individual progress, illuminates clear pathways for learning and reduces distractions.
- *Recognizes that mistakes are valuable learning opportunities*
  - As progress is tracked and monitored, and misunderstandings are identified, students increasingly rely on self-correction and modification to strengthen learning.

Promoting the Development of Noncognitive, Social, and Emotional Skills

- *Adjusts mindsets*
  - Students can be encouraged to change thinking from "I can't" to "Hey, I did better the second time." With increasing confidence, students can reroute attitudes from defiance to alliance, disorientation to comprehension, and compliance to autonomy.
- *Leads to higher levels of accountability*
  - Choice, ownership, and self-assessment put students at the helm. When they take responsibility for their learning outcomes, they become more self-reliant lifelong learners.
- *Builds self-advocacy*
  - When students understand the purposes, causes, and effects of an action, they are in a stronger position to speak out for themselves. As students mature, they find the words to ask for something to be repeated, explore options and opportunities, and explain feelings. Developing self-advocacy becomes a two-way street, as it also strengthens self-confidence.
- *Encourages a creative outlook*
  - Students are inspired to creatively think through choices and track their self-selected learning goals. They consider alternative or modified routes to their goals.
- *Boosts perseverance*
  - When students monitor their own learning, they observe their step-by-step progress, and in turn their ability to sustain learning increases.

Turning Engagement into Ownership

Being involved in learning and assessment is important. Ownership and personal responsibility are essential. It goes from making learning interesting to making learning meaningful. Parabolas may not be the most exciting concept in science but next time you are in Greenland, visit the Ameralik Span. This electrical overhead powerline is 5,376 meters long; it sags but never touches the ground. Using examples like this can turn parabolas and other challenges into real-world concepts, situations, and solutions.

Empowering students as assessors begins with an understanding and analysis of the design of the powerline. Then students explain the design by illustrating and modeling the scientific concepts that support it. For engagement, students use different lengths and materials to make their spans for analysis and comparison.

For younger learners, learning about the sequence of the butterfly lifespan also begins with observations of the process. They then learn the names of the stages and understand that all animals have a lifecycle. In turn, this leads to students illustrating the stages or making environmental recommendations for protecting butterflies.

The transition from engagement to ownership is summarized in table 6.1. It necessitates changes to teaching and also modifications to learning. Think about grade level and content areas where you can use this model. How can it help students choose healthy foods, understand percentages, or describe a virtual visit to an art museum?

Table 6.1. Making the Transition from Engagement to Ownership

	What the Teacher Does	What the Student Does
ENGAGEMENT	1. Conveys the goals in language understandable to students. 2. Plans learning and assessment actions that align with and lead to the learning intentions. 3. Motivates students through engagement and personalization.	1. Explains the purpose of learning in his or her own words. 2. Engages in meaningful learning experiences that align with the intentions. 3. Increases effort in response to improvement in understanding.
OWNERSHIP and EMPOWERMENT	1. Makes clear connections between learning sequence and outcomes. 2. Embeds assessments throughout learning. 3. Relies on multiple types of assessments. 4. Helps students see evidence of progress. 5. Transfers responsibility for learning and assessing to students.	1. Generates additional personalized learning aims, plans, and outcomes. 2. Uses evidence and feedback to guide modifications to learning. 3. Selects aligned and relevant ways to show what is learned. 4. Self-monitors progress. Sees the relationship of actions to outcomes. 5. Has multiple options for displaying his or her learning.

Student empowerment and ownership of assessment lead to a shared responsibility for learning. With constructive support and practical resources from teachers, students can successfully navigate through these stages of self- assessment:

- *Ownership, planning, action, and monitoring progress with support* is just one example that can be personalized for your school setting. For example, another sequence may include personalized learning objectives, strengthened decision-making skills, focused learning outcomes, improved self-reflection, and emphasized progress.
- *Ownership, planning, action, monitoring, and supporting* remain consistent whether engaging students in assessment, conveying ownership of assessment, or facilitating self-assessment. This sequence also provides the foundation for insightful and informative self- and peer assessment. When learners monitor their learning, they see step-by-step progress and in turn, their interest and ability for sustained learning increases.

Student ownership can be defined thus:

- Learning intentions and outcomes are clear from the start. Learners understand what and how they will be learning and why it is relevant and worthwhile.
- Assessments respect and respond to students' needs, interests, and abilities. For example, Bruno is excited when he learns he can pick which era and which president to research for his project. Bruno plans to present his research in a game format that he intends to align with the learning goals and rubric.
- Social and emotional skills are the foundation for progressing successfully toward personal mastery. For Murray, as he develops self-regulation, he notices that his grades also get better.

Students' ownership role includes the following steps:

1. Elaborate and personalize the learning intentions.
2. Understand the value of assessment data as well as descriptions of achievement.
3. Recognize the importance of noncognitive skills including intrapersonal awareness (i.e., self-regulation, mindset, and perseverance) and interpersonal understanding (i.e., perspective taking, collaboration, and conflict management).

Planning requires the following elements:

- Students translate big-picture goals into actionable achievement targets and learning routines. Jamal says, "I can sort statements into metaphors and similes and explain my thinking. Next, I'll try writing my own."
- Students understand the success criteria and how they will be assessed. They are informed consumers of the content, process, and strategies that are used to measure learning.

Students are expected to

- establish and individualize their own feasible and achievable learning targets;
- indicate the steps and time frame required to accomplish those aims;
- envision ways to display and assess their achievement of the learning intentions, which can include traditional, authentic, and original ways.

OWNERSHIP IN ACTION

Assessments measure a spectrum of learning outcomes from core knowledge to innovation. Planning is relevant to all subjects from astronomy to music. In art, Mr. Parisi uses content vocabulary and images to introduces styles of art. Students then select one period and produce their own example of art from that period. A rubric is used in the peer-review.

Students can learn to regulate their learning and determine their next steps. When students monitor their progress, they appreciate successes and take action on closing lingering gaps. Chara sees that she has missed a step in the learning progression. She knows that she must go back and check that she followed the correct sequence whether it be in her narrative, math problem, or photosynthesis.

Assessments are most effective when reciprocal, ongoing, and embedded throughout learning. Harriet explains, "In Mr. Jae's class, it's okay to make mistakes because they are opportunities for learning. It's way better than getting a bad grade at the end." Students can also utilize feedback that is focused, specific, and instructive. They respond by making adjustments to their learning. When Alef is given small chunks of feedback on specific learning aims, he quickly recognizes that he misunderstood step three in the formula.

When students are empowered, they

1. self-regulate their process, tempo, and depth of learning;
2. appropriately respond to difficulties and setbacks using problem solving and redirection;

3. recognize that mistakes are valuable learning opportunities;
4. take purposeful action on data, feedback, and other evidence of learning.

Tracking and Monitoring Progress

While assessment is diagnostic as well as formative and summative, the emphasis should focus on progress and improvement, Coretta says "Each time I write a letter it gets better. Now my salutation, content, and closing are stronger than ever." Formative assessments help students know where they are at the beginning of learning, monitor progress throughout learning, and inform their steps in narrowing their learning gaps and clarifying misunderstandings. By using a learning tracker, Camille can see she confused the verb tense, so she goes back and corrects her work.

Assessments require students to think about and apply what they have learned. Answers that can be looked up are less significant than those requiring analysis, forming connections, and producing defensible solutions. Tracking progress provides opportunities for revision and improvement before the final score.

In this way, students can

1. monitor their own pace and progress toward their identified learning intentions;
2. track their learning using data records and annotated learning progressions;
3. recognize the value of assessments that extend their thinking beyond knowledge and understanding and into analysis, evaluation, and production.

Ongoing support and guidance from instructional resources, peers, and the teacher are essential in developing assessment-capable learners. Access to resources is vital. Focused feedback and opportunities to modify work with accompanying explanations of what, how, and why they made the changes also are important. Fredericka gains little insight from a score of 71 percent on her quiz. She prefers support on the concepts she didn't understand and guidance on fixing her mistakes. When learning and assessment are meaningful, useful, and appropriately challenging, it not only reinforces learning but also makes learning endure. When Chan explains how Zoa can correct her graph, he is also deepening his own understanding.

Reframing opportunity as ownership means that students clearly understand the learning intentions, and now have the privilege and responsibility for fine-tuning and personalizing the learning goals. For some, this may mean deconstructing the goal into smaller and more achievable steps and for others adjusting the depth or breadth of the goal.

In the last chapter, we considered the practices and processes of student engagement in assessment. In this chapter, there was greater emphasis on students' owning the assessment. As you look through the example in table 6.2, consider Sasha's plan for learning and assessing. Notice how the integrity of her goal remains consistent while she also personalizes and deepens learning.

The plan for student ownership begins with student understanding and interpreting the learning intentions. Sasha has applied the model to her understanding of equivalent fractions. As you read, consider how you can adapt it for your grade level and content area. Table 6.2 can be used to rate your students' current level of expertise and implementation of the elements. Include evidence in your ratings. Envision where you would like to move the meter on each assessment standard. For each standard, identify actions you will take to move to your desired level of proficiency for empowering students as assessors.

Table 6.2. Developing Assessment-Capable Learners

Indicators of Assessment-Capable Learners	Current Status	Desired Level	Actions We Will Take
EXAMPLE: Student Ownership Students have opportunities for voice and choice in explaining learning intentions and displaying learning outcomes.	2–3	4	Teachers' Plan (generic example) We will begin with these three steps: 1. Identify incoming knowledge and skills and the supports and exemplars that students need to identify and personalize their learning intentions. 2. With students, brainstorm ways to display levels of achievement of the learning intentions. 3. Customize the SMART goals rubric for our grade level, content area, and students.
Own it: Understand learning intentions, expectations, and assessments. Recognize their role in successful outcomes.			Sasha's Plans for Equivalent Fractions My parents tried to help me understand equivalent fractions, but their old-fashioned way is different than how we learn in class. I'll try my teacher's suggestion of using visual representations, a tutorial, and some practice tests to get better at solving real-world problems using equivalent fractions.
Plan it: Develop learning targets, success criteria, steps, and timeline.			I used the SMART goals planner and began by taking apart the big picture standard, then chose a *Strategic Goal*. I will use models to display and explain equivalent fractions that are *Measurable*. I'm aiming for 85 percent on the unit assessment that we'll all take.

(continued)

Table 6.2. (continued)

Indicators of Assessment-Capable Learners	Current Status	Desired Level	Actions We Will Take
Take action: Self-regulate, solve problems, and utilize mistakes for improvement.			I found a great Khan Academy tutorial and will also use the flashcards on *Quizlet*. I can use that site to make my own flashcards that my classmates can also use to review and give me feedback on the accuracy and clarity of the questions on the cards.
Track it: Monitor, track, and extend learning.			Each day, as I take a practice assessment, I will note my progress and ask for help with things I still don't understand or am unable to do.
Be supported: Receive resources, feedback, and collaboration.			My teacher will help me choose helpful resources for the ideas I do not yet understand. He may pair me with peers who already get it.

REMINDER: The current level and desired level can be customized to specific learning intentions:

4 = Highly Capable, 3 = Generally Proficient, 2 = Working toward Competence, 1 = Room for Growth

Alternative Ranking

4 = Well above Average, 3 = Satisfactory Competence, 2 = Emerging Skills, 1 = Insufficient Evidence

Notes and comments:

As with other elements of supporting learners toward ownership of assessment, the teacher guides Sasha in her analysis of her plan when using the SOAR model in table 6.3.

Table 6.3. SOAR Analysis of Sasha's Use of the Empowerment Model

Acronym	Indicates/ Represents	In Practice
S	Student Standards Strategies	Sasha showed understanding of the topic by explaining the different ways that it can be taught. She explained her comprehension of the learning intentions in a way that gives her a relevant starting point for learning. She demonstrates her awareness of the standards as well as strategies to achieve them by explaining them in her own words.
O	Ownership Organization Onus	Sasha shows multiple indicators of ownership as she recognizes that there are different ways to learn about equivalent fractions. She uses and personalizes the SMART goal format to organize and sequence her own learning.
A	Agency Accountability Achievement	She shows awareness of the usefulness of formative assessment and feedback by combining tutorials with her development of flashcards. She recognizes the ways that her teachers can support and guide her self-regulated learning.
R	Results Review Respond	Tracking her progress is an essential element of quality assessment. It requires the ability to learn from mistakes and make steady progress in mastering the standards. Before she completes her learning, she reviews her progress and outcomes with her teacher.

The examples in the book are designed to be brief explanations and illustrations of practice. They are also intended to be descriptive rather than prescriptive. It is more important that teachers and students take time to reflect and respond to the concepts than feel pressured to hastily complete them. Think about how you can include this process to support and inform. Use table 6.4 for personal review, a one-to-one discussion, in small groups, as a whole class, or with a team.

Table 6.4. Reflection on Students' Ownership of Learning

REFLECT on the indicators of assessment-capable learners and answer the following questions.

Indicators of Assessment-Capable Learners	What Is the Evidence?
Own it: What is the evidence of student ownership and responsibility for their learning and assessment?	
Plan it: What steps and outcomes did the students identify in their learning plan?	
Take action: How clear, aligned, and feasible are the actions with the learning intentions and plans?	
Track it: What do you want to add to the students' notations about tracking learning? Are there other ways you will monitor progress?	
Be supported: How well do the resources support the students' learning plan? What is their strategy when they need help?	
ENRICHMENT *to extend learning:* What connections can they make to extend learning beyond the facts and understandings of the topic?	

Summarize your reflection, analysis, and recommendations for adjusting this process to best meet the needs of your students.

Before following the pathways for developing students as self-assessors, teachers must confirm that students feel safe, are healthy, and prepared to succeed in school and life. Students are less successful when they are malnourished, tired, scared, and disengaged. Assessment-proficient learners as well as their teachers must begin their journey with an understanding of what will be assessed, how, and why.

Think about It

Table 6.5 includes the sequences and steps that are the underpinnings of engaging learners in assessment and empowering them as assessors. Review the indicators, and rate your students' current level of expertise and implementation of the elements. Include evidence in your ratings. This can be done by and for individual learners or the whole class. Envision where you would like to move the meter on each assessment standard. For each standard, identify actions you and/or your students will take to move to your desired level of proficiency.

Table 6.5. Developing Engaged Learners and Assessors

Indicators of Assessment-Capable Learners	Current Status	Desired Level	Actions We Will Take to Develop These Skills in Our Students
EXAMPLE: Student Opportunity Students have opportunities for voice and choice in explaining learning intentions and displaying learning outcomes. *Opportunity*: Students understand learning intentions, expectations, and assessments. They recognize their role in successful outcomes. *Plan it*: Students develop/adapt learning targets, success criteria, steps, and timeline. *Take action:* Students self-regulate, solve problems, utilize mistakes for improvement, and are purposeful. *Track progress*: Students monitor, track, and extend learning. *Supported:* Students utilize resources, feedback, and collaboration.	2–3	4	In our first year, we will engage students in deconstructing learning standards into actionable learning intentions so they can show their understanding and explore ways to personalize learning.

4 = Highly Capable, 3 = Generally Proficient,
2 = Working toward Competence, 1 = Room for Growth
Notes and comments:

Chapter Seven

When Students Become Agents of Assessment

Figure 7.1. Walt Disney Concert Hall

Not every person has the same kinds of talents, so discover what yours are and work on them.

—Frank Gehry

"An agent is a person or thing that takes an active role or produces a specified effect" (Dictionary.com). In addition to being engaged, an empowered

brain takes responsibility for owning the assessment. Students become agents of assessment when they are actively involved in summarizing, elaborating, and organizing ideas through multiple methods and mediums. Empowered learners have opportunities to design assessments as well as adapt or customize assessment tasks.

Agents of assessment transform assessment from something that is conveyed to them to taking an active role. *Austin's Butterfly* is an inspiring video that demonstrates how descriptive feedback and support lead to improvement. When students were asked about ways to get to school, they said, "Take the bus or get a ride." When the teacher demonstrated a pogo stick and asked if anyone has a kayak, they began to joyfully propose using a zip line, snowmobile, and camel.

Beyond being motivated, agents of assessment use metacognitive strategies to monitor and modify learning. This is exemplified as first graders are testing their hypothesis on why things float or sink, and Milne observes, "My grandpa floats in the pool and my grandma sinks. I wonder why." Or middle school students consider reasons for changing Columbus Day to Indigenous Peoples Day, and Hector asks, "Why can't we do both?" and Geraldine says, "Let's find out what it takes to start a new holiday."

The caveat is that *not everyone* will, can, or should take agency all the time. Sometimes we don't know enough, or there is someone with more skills than we have, or we need to simply follow for our own good. Few of us can master a multifaceted standard in a predetermined period of time by using a single prescribed strategy. Think about how you learned to drive a car, or prepare healthy meals, or manage your money. Did you rely on expert guidance or trial and error, or perhaps some combination of both?

Standards are regularly accompanied by explicit instructional strategies for the teacher; resources for the student; opportunities for practice; and, more often than not, traditional measures. Very few standards are mono-dimensional offering one path for learning and a specific assessment. In general, standards such as these two large-scale ones, offer multiple opportunities to deconstruct, engage learners, and empower them as assessors:

- "Read closely to determine what the text says explicitly and to make logical inferences from it; cite specific textual evidence when writing or speaking to support conclusions drawn from the text."
- "Undertake a design project to construct, test, and modify a device that either releases or absorbs thermal energy through a chemical process."

Agency and ownership are important throughout life for many reasons. Think about any path in life from learning a new hobby to earning an advanced degree to being a compassionate caregiver. It is also essential to becoming our best selves. Based on the positive outcome research of Ronald Ferguson et al. (2015), here are some of the documented benefits of student agency and ownership in assessment and life:

1. Increased conscientiousness and responsibility
2. Active engagement in learning
3. Deeper insight into their own learning
4. Improved decision-making skills
5. More accurate monitoring of learning
6. Analysis of and learning from mistakes
7. Recognition and appreciation of personal growth
8. Learners become resources for each other
9. Development of self-confidence
10. Increased self-awareness along with fewer comparisons to others

ASSESSMENT THROUGH A STUDENT'S LENS

It takes time, preparation, and experience for teachers to cultivate their assessment skills. They may rely on their own school experiences, learn the basics in their teacher preparation programs, practice in their student-teaching experiences, and ultimately combine this with their school's expectations and requirements. Students also need to learn and practice self-assessment skills.

The fundamentals of developing assessment-capable learners include clarity and transparency, personal relevance, appropriate challenge, choice, and an emphasis on progress. The requisite skills are not only cognitive but also rely on non-cognitive foundations in support of self-confidence, motivation, self-regulation, meta-cognition, accountability, adaptability, problem solving, and communication. Interpersonal skills such as teamwork, compromise, empathy, fairness, and perspective taking also contribute to assessment efficacy.

Attributes of Quality Assessments

Consider the following attributes of quality assessments and the students' words in explaining each:

- *Clarity and Transparency Strategies*
  - Align standards and learning intentions with learning outcomes and products.

- Offer opportunities for students to display their learning through a range of strategies from traditional tests to alternative assessments.
- Use evidence from a range of strategies from traditional tests to alternative measures.
- Include focused targets, structured sequences, and defined roles for collaborative learning.
- Prepare students for peer reviews that are specific, actionable, and focused on improvement.

- *Clarity in Student's Words*

  "We're going to learn about the history of early European settlers: why they came, how they lived, and who they fought with. I know there will be a typical quiz with each part of the unit (i.e., colonies, expansion, disputes, and wars). For the project, I would like to work with Ab, and Cy to design a map of expansion using Nat-Geo Mapmaker. This will be scored by my classmates for accuracy, details, and visual elements."

- *Relevance Options*
  - Encourage students to make personal connections that give meaning to learning.
  - Provide personalized feedback input from multiple assessors: teacher, self, and peers.
  - Incorporate clear and relevant assessment criteria.
  - Emphasize real-world applications of learning.

- *Relevance in Student's Words*

  "I never liked science much, but if we're making kites to learn about *lift, drag, and gravity*, then I'm all in. I want to make the most beautiful kite that is decorated with explanations and diagrams of those three key terms. In that way, I will learn how to be an artist while doing it. I'll assess how well my kite flies by timing it and see how high it goes. Then I'll use the vocabulary to explain what happened and use suggestions from my teacher and peers to make it better next time."

- *Appropriate Challenges*
  - Consider the level of difficulty: seek a balance between frustration/overwhelmed and boredom/underwhelmed.
  - Match the challenge with the students' skills.
  - Support students in planning their steps toward success.
  - Incorporate a fair and balanced continuum of instructive assessments from formative to summative.

- *Appropriate Challenge in Student's Words*

  "Sometimes school seems so hard. I missed a lot of days in my old school and am trying to catch up this year. My teacher has been really helpful in helping me deconstruct (I like that word!) the goals so that

I understand them. If I get stuck, I sometimes work with Janna, who's pretty smart. I like to record my answers rather than write them down as my handwriting stinks."

- *Choices*
  - Engage students in multiple pathways for monitoring and displaying learning.
  - Include students in the design and methods of local assessments.
  - Integrate non-cognitive skills, such as personal responsibility and reflective listening.
  - Offer and encourage students' accurate and insightful revisions of work.
- *Choices in Student's Words*
  "When I started this year I hated to write, really hated it. In my other school, we were given boring topics like how I felt about stuff and things my family didn't do, like celebrate holidays. This year, my teacher gives us a choice of topics to write about as long as we meet the fourth-grade requirements for things like having a main idea, clarity, elaboration, spelling, and sentence structure."
- *Improvement/Progress*
  - Sequence learning intentions using competency-based progressions.
  - Seek evidence of reliance and responsiveness to informative assessment and feedback.
  - Involve students as analyzers of outcomes and data.
  - Verify ongoing progress as well as identify lingering gaps.
  - Identify the types of statements that can help students understand that their progress outplays final scores.
- *Progress in Student's Words*
  "Shazam! Tracking and reflecting on my learning really does work. Each time I looked at my scores, they got better. That's because I was able to identify what I understood and what I need to work on. And, each color in the red, yellow, green flow chart included a review, helpful hints, and practice exercises."

Empowering Students as Designers of Assessment

The following examples illustrate how the development and support of assessment-capable learners can be integrated into daily routines of learning.

- *Clarity:* Ms. Macri wants to engage middle school students in assessing this big-picture standard: "Determine central ideas of a text and explain how the author conveys their point of view. Use textual evidence." Lanika says, "I will read the Gettysburg Address and tell you when Lincoln wrote it, who he was speaking to, and how people reacted to it." Damon says, "I will read the Gettysburg Address, summarize three key ideas, record three persuasive phrases, and explain why Lincoln's ideas are still relevant today." Ramona says, "I will rewrite the Gettysburg Address to reflect today's political events, controversies, and contradictions."

- *Ms. Macri's Analysis of Clarity:* Lanika uses the words when, who, and how. These indicate more of a description of the document and less of an analysis of purpose and perspective. Damon uses the words summarize, main ideas, and persuasive phrases. Damon's learning intention is more closely matched to the standard. He is able to show understanding and interpretation in relation to his own learning intentions and actions. Ramona has reached beyond the standard by showing her understanding of political positions and controversies. Ms. Macri suggests that Lanika refers to the evidence she used to support her ideas.
- *Relevance:* Ms. Macri notes that some students are developing understanding by creating a narrative of the war from a northern or southern perspective. Others are ready for extending their learning. They compare the Gettysburg Address to Martin Luther King's "I Have a Dream" speech or another historical speech of their choosing. As the unit moves forward, students quiz each other on the vocabulary of the speeches (i.e., proposition, endure, hallowed) using a formative assessment when self-correcting their work.
- *Reasonable Challenge:* Lanika is advised to deconstruct the goal into three main ideas and then describe her own learning intentions. Relying on an exemplar and feedback, she rewrites it like this: "I will start by rereading the Gettysburg address, underlining the main ideas, and circling persuasive words such as self-evident and dedicate. Then in my summary, I will use those words and ideas to explain Lincoln's thinking and persuasive techniques." Once mastery of central ideas is demonstrated, the students are asked to explain the ideas to someone from another time period or debate whether this could happen today. They also can display their results on a graphic organizer, such as Canva or Popplet, explaining the political, economic, and social influences.
- *Choice:* Ms. Macri asks them how they can show deeper understanding beyond the vocabulary and ideas that Lincoln was expressing. In the past, she gave students three "points of view" statements, and each student selected one and explained how Lincoln used words and imagery to support his ideas. She decides to offer other options for showing their learning. In small groups, they brainstorm ideas such as put on a play, compare it to other presidential addresses (e.g., FDR's 1933 Inauguration speech), or write a letter to the editor on a current issue in the style of the Gettysburg address.

- *Improvement/Progress:* Students use learning trackers to annotate progress as well as challenges. They seek help from additional resources as needed, from peers as relevant, and from the teacher as necessary. The students have agreed to use the teacher's designed rubric for now. Scoring is based on their understanding of content, summary, analysis of a position, and use of evidence to support ideas.

Table 7.1. SOAR Analysis of Student Agency

Acronym	Indicates/ Represents	In Practice
S	Student Standards Strategies	The students translated the big-picture standard and goal into actionable learning intentions. Their depth of thinking reflected their individual proficiency levels while reaching ahead. The goal and strategy become more evident as they develop their learning plan with the teacher's support.
O	Ownership Organization Onus	Each student defined and formatted his or her learning in a way that is meaningful and relevant to his or her skills and interests. At the same time, this leads to higher levels of engagement. The teacher guides and focuses each student's learning.
A	Agency Appraisal Achievement	Student choice is evident in explicit learning plans. Students own the learning but also recognize the value of feedback in raising their levels of achievement. The scoring method and criteria are consistent across projects while being relevant to varied learning paths toward the goal.
R	Results Review Respond	Students adjusted their learning as they tracked their progress. Their ownership resulted in more complex and comprehensive learning than if the teacher followed a prescribed lesson plan. As students explained, they were motivated to keep learning, yet were adaptable in their process.

Ms. Macri asked her students for feedback on their learning. They suggested that additional scoring criteria such as originality and collaboration should be included. They rated the unit as high on engagement, personal relevance, and depth of learning, but made recommendations for a clearer sequence and more flexible timeframe next time.

Think about It

Discuss the following questions with your team. Use your collective ideas to develop an action plan for your own setting.

1. With your team, select a grade-level standard to deconstruct so that it is specific, accurate, clear, and understandable to your students.
2. How can you support students in translating these learning intentions into actionable plans?
3. What modifications can be made so that each student has a personally meaningful, developmentally appropriate, and achievable goal?
4. In what ways is it feasible to include student choice in the process and products of learning?
5. How can you translate this into a progress tracker so that each student can monitor, record, and evaluate the steps they are taking?
6. What opportunities can you incorporate for self-reflection, peer review, and teacher feedback?
7. How will the student process and outcomes be scored, graded, and reported?
8. In general, how can you incorporate the SOAR model in your planning, teaching, and student learning? How might you adapt it?

STRATEGIES THAT EMPOWER STUDENTS AS ASSESSORS: CHOICE, VOICE, COURSE

When students are engaged *in* assessment, they have a role in selecting the assessments, monitoring progress, and adjusting their learning process. When they have a role *as* assessors, they are planning, learning, and displaying their outcomes. Personalizing the learning tasks and assessments is an essential element of ownership. Directions in a guidebook or steps in a recipe may seem clear, until students are expected to turn north, or blanch the vegetables, or don't understand the meaning in step 3. Even clear directions can get derailed as students find themselves getting sidetracked.

Mr. Golden understands this, so he begins most units with a pre-assessment. He may use a quick quiz using Google Forms or electronic sticky notes such as lino (http://en.linoit.com/). Mr. Golden notices that collectively students can define DNA, RNA, chromosomes, and mutation, but have less familiarity with the transmission of genetic defects. He decides to start with a brief review in small groups of students with mixed abilities. In this way, he is starting where his students are, reviewing prior learning, and getting them ready to construct new understandings. Once the groundwork is put in place, he considers ways to engage learners as assessors throughout teaching and learning.

Assessments can be like rainbows. They may come in different sizes and clarity, yet all rely on the same spectrum of colors in reflecting the sun's light. Like rainbows, there are also multiple ways for students to show and reflect what they know about a character's motives, healthy eating, fractions, or global languages. Below are examples of varied and personalized paths for demonstrating intentional learning followed by methods that encourage accurate self-assessment:

Choice: The importance of choice was introduced in the previous chapter as a strategy for engagement. Choice also empowers students with options for displaying learning processes and outcomes through progressions and taxonomies. For example, Janessa knows that topical vocabulary will be assessed with quickie quizzes throughout learning, but she is also aware that there will be opportunities to demonstrate her ability to apply and display her understanding through media and other artifacts. Table 7.2 shows how choices can support standards and also align with progress through the taxonomy. Table 7.3 shows how this can be extended by incorporating point values into the options.

Table 7.2. Assessment Choice Board

Vocabulary Development	*Vocabulary Expansion*	*Vocabulary Mastery*
Write down the vocabulary words then compose an original sentence using them.	Write a letter explaining the vocabulary to someone who has no experience with it.	Create a graphic organizer that extends the basic terminology into more descriptive and complex vocabulary.
Match vocabulary to illustrations. Explain your thinking.	Ed Puzzle: Watch a video. Record and evaluate the use of the content vocabulary in helping the viewer understand its meaning.	Produce a video tutorial on the content vocabulary. Include examples to expand the viewers' understanding.
Quizlet or Quizziz: Review vocabulary in a multiple choice quiz format.	Create flash cards with synonyms or illustrations of the vocabulary.	Write a short story or test questions that show your understanding of the terminology.

Table 7.3. Weighted Choice Board

Points/Level of Learning	Choice 1	Choice 2	Choice 3
3 Points Recall and Understand	Arrange puzzle pieces of the story into the correct sequence.	Illustrate/write the three steps for making playdough.	Write questions to use in a peer review of new vocabulary.
6 Points Scrutinize, Analyze, and Apply	Develop and add a new character. Explain his purpose and influence on the storyline.	Defend how your notes and resources align with the learning targets.	Explore experts' solutions to a problem. Design a pros/cons graphic.
9 Points Synthesize and Create	Design a sales campaign to sell your story to a publisher.	Design a game to help others review their learning.	Develop and defend an original solution to a problem.

Voice: Voice means that students have opportunities to express preferences and share perspectives. It also means listening carefully to what another is saying. A clear and focused voice is important for all students, from those with quiet voices to those who have found a voice that is loud and persistent. For many students, thinking out loud builds stronger connections to learning. In relation to assessment, students can be given voice by intentionally asking them for their thoughts, ideas, and experiences on topics and assessments as in the following examples:

- What types of assessments are you most successful with?
- What do you find most challenging about tests and assessments?
- What do you find fair and unfair about tests and assessments?
- What opportunities do I have to ask questions about the teacher's assessment and grading in general?
- What occasions are there for me to ask about specific questions on a test?
- How can I annotate my tests with questions, comments, and suggestions?

In turn, voice leads to higher levels of engagement and greater ownership of learning and outcomes.

Students' Assessment of Their Learning Outcomes: Students can use phrases on the list below, or generate their own responses to their lingering gaps and points of confusion. Later, this can be used to review a test or assignment that has been scored and returned.

- "I made a simple mistake with ____. Next time I will ____."
- "I was absent the day we learned and practiced this skill. Are there any review sheets?"
- "The words in the question confused me. I think I could give a better answer if I understood what regulated and militia mean."
- "The school I came from didn't teach the background information I need for this question. Where's Oregon?"

Engaged students are motivated to achieve their best. When considering student success indicators, engaged and motivated students have

- the ability to persevere when challenges occur;
- optimism when talking about goals;
- a balance of sleep, healthy eating, exercise, and extracurricular activities;
- appropriate study skills for learning new and challenging content;
- critical thinking skills for making difficult choices.

Students' Tracking Progress: There are multiple models for tracking numerical scores. Traditional charts and graphs may be easy to use, but they don't offer adequate insight into the causes and influences on learning outcomes. They may make it hard to tell whether the student is having a bad day, is perplexed by a learning strategy, or doesn't understand the learning intention. There are also numerous ways for students to chart their own scores.

Chapter 5 included students' assessment of their engagement. As agents of assessment, students also track their developing mastery, record quantitative progress, and assess qualitative outcomes. Students can start by developing a communal grid of the topic's goals. On it, each student records their individual learning intentions. A goal may be to develop conversational fluency about dining using another language. One student may want to record himself saying ten foods from the lesson and get suggestions for improvement in pronunciation from the teacher. Another student may prefer to have a conversation with one or two peers and receive feedback from them on the clarity of their interaction with the waiter and accurate use of vocabulary.

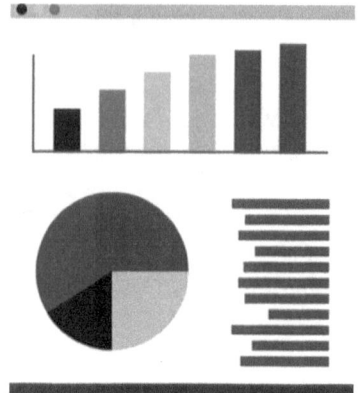
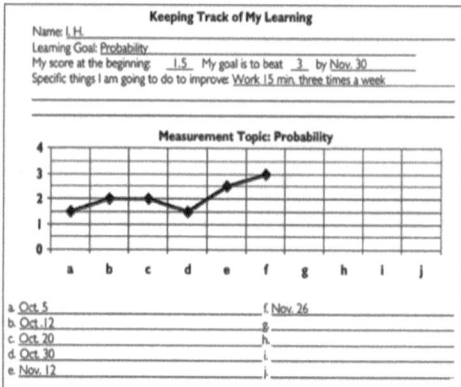

Figure 7.2.   Traditional graph   Figure 7.3.   Student as tracker

Course/Process: Relying on the essential elements of purposeful, planned, and sequenced assessment helps all students achieve. Pre-assessments, formative assessments, personalized assessments, and summative assessments are all essential. As engagement broadens into empowerment, student ownership of assessment also increases from

- taking tests *to* writing test questions;
- filling in answers *to* annotating tests and assessments;
- broad spectrum standards *to* personalized learning intentions;
- explicit teaching and testing *to* self-directed learning and assessment;
- receiving ideas/instruction *to* developing insight;
- receiving feedback *to* sharing insights;
- collecting final scores *to* monitoring progress;
- teacher control of testing *to* student-designed assessments;
- final scores *to* opportunities for improvement.

The SMART goal model introduced in chapter 2 and summarized in table 2.1 is elaborated in table 7.4. SMART is an easy-to-use and consistent strategy for empowering students as assessors. The processes of Specific, Measurable, Attainable, Relevant, and Time-Based have broad applications. For some students, the vocabulary can be simplified, from Specific to Clear and from Attainable to Doable. The model is relevant for all learners by further adjusting the language levels. For example, "What are my explicit goals?" is simplified to "This is what I want to learn." "What actions and steps will I take?" translates to "My first step will be."

Personalization of goals starts with each student's incoming knowledge and skills and present position on the learning path. In this way, competition is reduced (and thus stress) and is refocused on personal achievement by asking each student to consider his or her inbound knowledge and skills in relation to learning intentions and outcomes. Once students become familiar with the model, they can use it to plan and track their own learning. Table 7.4 shows how Tomas has personalized his SMART goals.

Table 7.4. SMART Goals in a Student's Words

Goal	Planning: Questions to Consider in Setting Goals	Outcomes, Evidence, and Reflections: In Student's Words
S SPECIFIC AND STRATEGIC	What do I plan on learning? How well will my plans lead to the goal? How will I know when I am successful?	Goals: I want to be able to order dinner at a Spanish restaurant. I now know 8 food words and when I learn 30 more, I will be able to order accurately. Success Criteria: I will be served the chorizo not the cochinillo.
M MEASURABLE AND MOTIVATIONAL	How will I know how well I achieved each goal? What evidence of achievement do I need? What qualitative and quantitative data are required?	I will accurately pay the equivalent of euros in dollars. My peers will check my math. I want to achieve 90 percent accuracy.
A ACTIONABLE AND ACHIEVABLE	What do I want and need to know and do? What actions and steps will I take? How realistic/feasible are these plans?	I will learn about the customs in Spanish restaurants. My peers will give me feedback on my manners and my ordering. They will offer suggestions for improvement. I will record my experience for my teacher to assess.
R RELEVANT AND REALISTIC	How does this build on my prior learning and support future learning? How will I be able to use my learning in and beyond the classroom?	After 8th grade, my family is going on a trip to my grandparents' country. I want to be able to order food for them when we are there.
T TIME-BASED AND TANGIBLE	What is a feasible timetable for completing my plan? How can I monitor and make certain that I will stick to the plan?	I will work on this goal during this school year and monitor my progress with a rubric for accuracy and the number of newly learned vocabulary words. When I reach my goal, I will bring churros for my whole class. If I don't achieve the goal, my family will be disappointed.

STUDENTS AS ASSESSORS OF THEIR OWN LEARNING

All students are capable of self-assessment. Watch an infant who wants something that is just out of reach. The child will try all kinds of stretching motions and attention-getting noises until the object is in hand, often accompanied by a self-assured smile or coo. As children grow, those who can accurately define a problem, try out alternative strategies, revise those attempts, and ultimately achieve success, are developing skills that will serve them throughout their lifetime.

Too often, educators believe they need to be in charge of assessment. And too often, especially in a testing-based educational system, the onus for student success is placed in teachers' hands. In developing students as assessors of their own learning, responsibility is transferred, step by step, from readiness to engagement to ownership and agency.

Assessment of Student Understanding through Ownership and Agency

Here is a sequence for students to use or adapt to show their step-by-step progress.

1. I'm not sure I know and understand it yet. It's not really clear enough for me to take action.
   - Here is what I do not understand.
   - Here are the questions I have.
2. I am starting to understand the topic and ideas in general.
   - I am doing okay with _____.
   - I still need help with _____.
3. I understand what I am supposed to be learning and can usually do it by myself.
   - I can show what I am learning.
   - Sometimes I ask the teacher or a classmate to clarify how and what we are learning and doing.
4. Assessment of student ownership and agency is demonstrated through a student's reflections and actions.
   - I understand and show what I know and can do in various ways such as orally, in writing, or a diagram.
   - For the most part, I can teach someone else what I have learned.
   - Sometimes I can think of other ways to learn more about it or accomplish it independently.

Examples of students' assessment and analysis of learning outcomes can include the following:

1. My score or rating was _____.
2. Here is the evidence/explanation of why I earned that score _____.
3. I did best on _____.
4. It looks like I still need help with _____.
5. Here's the level I would like to be at _____.
6. These are some steps I can take to improve _____.

Think about It through Two Lenses

First, a case study is provided from a teacher's perspective followed by students' musings about their own motivation, mindset, and accountability. How would these be adaptable and beneficial in your own setting?

Case Study: Burning Both Ends of the Candle

There's a new principal at West End Elementary School. She's fresh from a doctoral program in educational leadership with prior teaching experience at a small K–8 school. Due to budget constraints and hiring delays, she is starting her employment on the first day of school. Her welcoming message emphasizes her core beliefs:

- All students can learn—in their own way at their own pace.
- Attending to the development of the whole child is essential for their academic success.
- Progress is a more powerful motivator than a final score.
- When we work as a team, we are more capable than when we work in isolation.

Her message about learning and assessing is more comprehensive. It is based on the belief that students learn best in active, engaging environments. Formative practices can personalize learning and strengthen outcomes for all learners, and even the youngest students can be taught to communicate effectively, think critically, and act creatively. She explains that she does not intend to micro-manage classrooms, but rather is looking for outcomes. These outcomes include visible evidence of engaged learners, opportunities for each student to improve, and effective routines of assessment of these outcomes.

She asks each teacher team to review and think about ways to adapt one unit for a lesson study experience. In two weeks, the teachers will be expected to bring a current curriculum to begin the process of strengthening assessments. She encourages the teachers to bring elements of the redesign and examples in practice and to expect feedback and guidance on their ideas. Describe what your team of teachers will present to the faculty in a few weeks. Examples include:

- Suggest changes to the curriculum to make sure that all students are assessment ready.
- Identify practices that will engage students in assessment.
- Describe ways to transfer ownership and empower students as assessors.
- Illuminate your thought processes and explain how these practices support the engagement and empowerment of students in assessment.

Check-in on Student Motivation, Mindset, and Accountability

Motivation: Motivation is an underlying principle of student ownership and agency for learning and assessing. Table 7.5 asks students to reflect and self-assess their assessment readiness skills. (Note that the sequence progress is from 5 for highly motivated and capable to 1 for unmotivated and inexperienced.)

Table 7.5. Student Reflection and Motivation

Think about each of these statements in relation to your typical behaviors. Then select the words from the 5 to 1 scale to express your beliefs and actions.

5. Strongly Agree, Almost Always; 4. Agree, Often; 3. Unsure, Sometimes; 2. Disagree, Once in a While; 1. Strongly Disagree, Never or Hardly Ever

1. I can set realistic goals for myself and my learning.	5	4	3	2	1
2. I am confident that I can achieve my goals.	5	4	3	2	1
3. Even when learning is hard, I am willing to try my best. I believe that with hard work I can be successful.	5	4	3	2	1
4. Usually, I have a pretty good idea of what I am expected to do and learn.	5	4	3	2	1
5. When I face unexpected challenges, I continue to work at it.	5	4	3	2	1
6. I work at monitoring my progress so I can make adjustments along the way.	5	4	3	2	1
7. I seek help when I face difficulties and encounter obstacles to learning.	5	4	3	2	1
8. I set targets for myself that are feasible but I am also willing to stretch my knowledge and skills.	5	4	3	2	1
9. When I complete an assignment successfully, I am really surprised.	5	4	3	2	1
10. I focus more on why something won't work or why I can't do it.	5	4	3	2	1
11. I do my work to avoid negative consequences.	5	4	3	2	1
12. Sometimes, I just don't understand what I am expected to do.	5	4	3	2	1
13. After a while, if I can't do it, I simply give up.	5	4	3	2	1

Add your thoughts, experiences, insights, explanations, and reasoning:

Mindset: In addition to readiness, student's also need the right mindset to be successful in their learning. Supporting and developing growth mindsets in learners can make a significant difference in learning outcomes. Use table 7.6 to rate yourself on a 1 to 5 scale, with 5 meaning you agree wholeheartedly and 1 meaning you disagree strongly. Clarify your thoughts in the reflection section. Select one or two of the criteria to develop an action plan. (Note that the beliefs and actions alternate between a growth and fixed mindset.)

Table 7.6. Mindset Reflection for Students

Think about each of these statements in relation to your typical behaviors. Then select the words from a 5 to 1 scale to express your beliefs and actions.
5. Strongly Agree, Almost Always; 4. Agree, Often; 3. Unsure, Sometimes; 2. Disagree, Once in a While; 1. Strongly Disagree, Never or Hardly Ever

Mindset Matters	Rating 5 4 3 2 1	Reflection/Description/ Explanation
1. I prefer school work that is challenging, so I can learn new things.		
2. Trying something new is stressful for me, so I avoid it.		
3. The harder you work at something, the better you will be at it.		
4. It is hard to change the basic things about the kind of person you are.		
5. I appreciate constructive feedback from coaches and teachers.		
6. I often get angry when people comment on my work or ideas.		
7. A person can be smart in one area but need to try harder in another.		
8. Compared to others, I am usually smarter and more knowledgeable.		
9. I work hard even when I don't like the subject or the work.		
10. If you are smart, you shouldn't have to work hard.		

STEPS IN CREATING AN ACTION PLAN in response to your reflection. For each item you want to act on: 1. Describe the current status. 2. Clarify how you would like it to be. 3. Explain two adjustments you can make or actions you can take, to help you move toward step 2. 4. How will you monitor your progress? 5. How will you assess success?	YOUR PLAN 1. 2. 3. 4. 5.

Accountability: By now you have an understanding of the importance of student agency in assessment as well as perspectives on ways to convey this responsibility. Table 7.7 has some ideas that teachers and students can use for assessing student accountability for learning and assessment.

Table 7.7. Accountability Rubric

Skill/Knowledge	EXEMPLARY	PROFICIENT	DEVELOPING	NOVICE
Goal setting and action planning	Routinely develops realistic goals and actionable steps	Defines a few goals and develops a basic plan to follow	Goals are partially formed and plans describe potential steps	Requires support in setting and working toward goals
Focus and follow through	Purposefully works toward goals and attentively implements plans	Follows the basic plan in order to achieve goals	Randomly works toward goals, but generally on a short-term basis	Focus and follow through on goals are imprecise
Personal responsibility	Demonstrates a high level of responsibility for self and effect of actions on others	Typically accepts responsibility for actions and recognizes this effect on others	With reminders can assume personal responsibility for actions	Has difficulty understanding the meaning of personal responsibility
Preparation and readiness	Prepared, organized, and conscientious learner who goes beyond requirements	Usually prepared for class and ready to learn without supervision to achieve goals	Partially prepared for class and requires some supervision to complete tasks	With assistance can complete assignments
Monitors and perseveres	Actively monitors learning and thoughtfully adapts to challenges	Keeps track of learning and works conscientiously	Recognizes that things are not moving forward and unmindful of what to do	Unaware of the pathways of learning and the effort required
Self-Assessment	Relies on process and outcomes when comparing personal work to success criteria	Considers the process and outcome in relation to criteria when self-assessing	Able to match learning outcomes to success criteria	Has difficulty comparing personal learning outcomes to the criteria
Outcomes	Effectively coordinates goals and plans to ensure quality products that exceed expectations	Willing to work toward goals and follows plans for effective productivity	Inconsistent adherence to goals and plans and compromises learning outcomes	Scarcity of interest results in substandard outcomes

Table 7.8. Self-Assessment of Personal Accountability

How I Demonstrate Accountability	5 = Always 4 = Mostly 3 = Sometimes 2 = Rarely 1 = Never	Explanation or Example of My Rating
1. I can deconstruct the learning objectives into feasible steps for me.		
2. I am able to develop my own learning intentions and action plan.		
3. I work on an assignment and follow through until it is done.		
4. If I get off track, I know how to move forward or find help.		
5. I can compare my work to the goals and success criteria.		
6. I know how to find accurate information to reach my goal.		
7. I use self-reflection and feedback to improve my work.		
8. I am successful in assessing my own work.		
9. If I am unable to reach my goals, I can explain what happened.		

Exit Slip: End-of-the-Lesson Reflection

- ✓ I demonstrated accountability when I _____.
- ✓ One thing that helps me be accountable is _____.
- ✓ I can do better in being accountable next time by _____.
- ✓ One thing that keeps me from being accountable is _____.
- ✓ Reflection and feedback help me be accountable by _____.
- ✓ What happened when I was not accountable for my actions? _____.

Team Accountability Cards: Before starting to work as a group, each member makes a statement about his or her accountability for completing the assignment. At the conclusion, the actions are verified and feedback is provided.

- ➢ When I find myself off-task I will _____.
- ➢ Today I will work on this goal by _____.
- ➢ It's okay to remind me to _____.
- ➢ For this project I will take responsibility for 1._____, 2._____, and 3._____.

Putting into Practice

This final section unifies numerous essential ideas from throughout the book. It is an example of a project where students are engaged as learners, become owners of their own assessments, and take responsibility for being agents and managers of their learning outcomes.

SAMPLE GRANT TEMPLATE FOR A THIRD-GRADE COMMUNITY SERVICE FIELD TRIP

Note: Grant question prompts included from a *Corwin Connect* blog post on *Empower Your Students to Design and Fund Their Own Project-Based Learning Experiences* (Burke, 2018).

Learning Outcome: By the end of the field trip, we will describe how a lack of trash management impacts land, water, and wildlife.

Selected Standards:
- Conduct short research projects that build knowledge about a topic.
- Write informative texts to examine a topic and convey ideas and information clearly.
- Produce writing in which the development and organization are appropriate to task and purpose.
- Write opinion pieces on topics of texts supporting a point of view with reasons.

Need Statement: Why does your class need to travel for this learning experience?
- *What project-based learning problem are you going to solve?*
- *What is your understanding of the problem?*

Our third-grade class is studying sea life. We want to participate in the Waterside State Park Junior Ranger Program that includes learning about how a poor trash management program hurts land, water, and wildlife.

Goal Statement: What is the goal of this project-based learning experience?
  I will explain how poor trash management hurts the environment especially the ocean, land, and wildlife at this park. I will observe and record what the park is doing to manage the trash problem. Then I will compare their process to my research on the best ways to manage trash according to my Junior Ranger Adventure Guide. These standards are included in my English, social studies, and science classes.

Objectives with activities, timeline, and how to measure results: What are the activities with timeline and evaluation for this field trip?
- *What are the steps you will use to solve the problem?*
- *Who are you collaborating with when resolving the problem?*
- *What is the feedback from the various stakeholders?*
- *What else should be asked to solve the problem?*
- *How will the team reflect on the problem-solving process?*
- *How will your team share their product and results?*
- *How can you ensure that your teacher can provide flexible choices?*

By (date), the class will travel to the state park and attend the Junior Ranger Program. We will learn how poor trash management affects land, water, and wildlife while we clean up the beach. When completing the *Junior Ranger Adventure Guide*, I can write a story about how a state park is protecting wildlife through the trash management program. The guide also provides a checklist of items that are harmful to wildlife. I can post this list at home and inspect my yard for any dangerous items that may harm birds and animals.

We will return our completed *Junior Ranger Adventure Guide* and bags of trash to the ranger. The park ranger will review our work and ask us questions. If we are successful, we will receive our junior ranger badges. My classmates will help us learn how to protect wildlife, recycle, and clean up the waterfront. Our teacher and the ranger will provide us with guidance as we plan for follow-up activities. They will provide us with feedback on our work and what we have learned. We will display our completed adventure guides on our class bulletin board for others to review how poor trash management hurts land, water, and wildlife.

Budget and Budget Narrative: What are the expenses that need funding for this trip?
- *What are the staffing costs?*
- *What are the fees for books, supplies, and equipment?*
- *What are the entrance fees for students?*
- *Are there other miscellaneous expenses?*

The budget for this activity includes a $5 fee per student for admission into the park and park materials. $100 is for transportation and snacks for participants. We will raise the money by writing and selling our own guide to protect the environment and sell reusable shopping bags.

When Students Become Agents of Assessment 105

Table 7.9. SOAR Analysis

Acronym	Indicates/ Represents	In Practice
S	Student Standards Strategies	Through their study of sea life, students demonstrated a good grasp of nature and ecology. They asked a series of relevant questions to inform and guide their intention of cleaning the waterfront. Suggestion: Students and teacher can work together to identify clear, actionable, and assessable standards and learning intentions.
O	Ownership Organization Onus	As they learned about nature, ecology, and recycling, they relied on valid information from the ranger to understand the importance of keeping their beaches clean. This led to their waterfront clean-up plans, a feasible schedule, and successful outcome.
A	Agency Accountability Achievement	Students were able to see progress as they tracked their work in the *Junior Ranger Adventure Guide* and also as the waterfront became visibly cleaner. Suggestion: Incorporate assessments that align with the goals. For example, include vocabulary knowledge, data on environmental damage, or collaborative problem-solving strategies. Engage students in deciding the best ways for them to display learning.
R	Results Review Respond	To interest other students in the topic, they posted their adventure guides in their school. Their detailed grant template resulted in funding for their project. It also expressed excitement about doing similar projects in the future to make the world a better place. What suggestions do you have for improving this project or using the ideas in your setting?

Think about It: Musings on Empowering Students as Assessors

Review the following steps for empowering students:

- STEP 1: Think about K–12 students and how they can design and participate in assessments. Consider the examples and ideas in this book that are relevant to your setting.
- STEP 2: Describe three steps you will take to engage and empower students as assessors. Example: The fifth-grade teachers reviewed their current curriculum in (subject) to look for evidence of ways that students

currently assess their own learning. They noted opportunities that are currently incorporated in each unit as examples of students self-correcting their weekly vocabulary. They will work together to identify additional opportunities and specify ways to expand students' self and peer assessment that supports the curriculum and learning.
- STEP 3: Consider the opportunities for developing students as agents of assessment.
- STEP 4: Consider any challenges you, your team, and students may face during this process. Anticipate how you will respond to them.

Part III

Chapter Eight

Partnering with Parents to Empower Students

Figure 8.1. Partnering with parents in support of learning

There are two things that we should give our children. One is roots and the other is wings.

—Attributed to many, from Wolfgang Goethe to Hodding Carter

Each child is unique yet follows similar sequences of development. As such, most curricula are designed to emphasize the fundamental concepts and norms for grade levels and content areas while keeping in mind the uniqueness of each student as well as the needs of schools, communities, and families. Here are some examples.

Brandon loves to write and is a huge fan of the *Captain Underpants* books. He spends time at school and home illustrating and writing new adventures of Captain Underpants as time allows. Mrs. Marcus, his teacher, reassures Brandon that he can share one of his favorite stories with the class during the transition to the next learning center activity if Brandon stays on task and satisfactorily completes his current math assignment. This compromise allows Brandon to excel at writing stories while also completing his required assignments in a satisfactory and timely manner. In this way, he is engaged through choice and empowered through sharing his creative ideas.

Rosie has been inspired by her brother to someday become a teacher who helps students with their individualized learning needs. She loves to work with her classmates during group projects and recognizes that each one has something special to contribute to the project. She also thinks it is important to hold each learner accountable and wants to devise an annotated checklist of each team member's contributions in group projects. Rosie agrees with her teacher that this engages her more deeply in the group work and also serves to monitor students and allow them to be responsible for their own progress.

These students have differing perspectives, needs, and interests, yet both are engaged in their classroom because their teacher has provided opportunities to use their talents and at the same time be empowered in their learning.

Mrs. Marcus also relies on parents and community volunteers in the classroom to help individuals as well as small groups of students. The teacher encourages these volunteers in using their strengths and interests to engage and support learners. Students also welcome the volunteers who come intentionally at specific times and days to help with identified needs. This type of consistent participation of specific teachers and volunteers in the classroom provides students with a sense of security while accommodating their diverse needs and engaging all learners.

TEACHER INITIATED ACTIVITIES THAT ENGAGE STUDENTS

Below are some examples of strategies to engage students and encourage higher levels of student ownership in learning and learning outcomes.

- Students share their work with peers using a structured feedback protocol. This motivates students and supports them as they productively contribute to learning.
- In small groups students read their journal or stories to each other, then receive encouragement and suggestions from other students in the group. Brainstorming ideas for the next part of a script, story, or opus, engages all students in learning while also empowering them to move forward with new ideas.
- Math teams coach each other when completing daily assignments and sharing insights on common challenges and strategies for success.
- After assignments are completed, students take "brain breaks" with a choice of activity. This could be a game or jumping jacks. Engagement is strengthened after a brain takes a rest.
- Collectively a class can develop classroom guidelines that support the success of each student. These can include clarifying expectations for communicating with others, seeking help, checking an assignment before turning it in, and assessing their use of time and materials.

Review the statements across each element of SOAR in table 8.1 and rate your readiness to partner with parents to support student engagement. In the recommendations section, include the steps that you can take to help parents understand the basics of engaging students in their learning at home.

OPPORTUNITIES TO PARTNER WITH PARENTS

As teachers become more familiar with the SOAR model of students as self-assessors, they have ample opportunities to share this model with families throughout the school year at:

- back-to-school meetings and activities;
- parent-teacher conferences;
- informal meetings with parents;
- parenting workshops;
- approved digital resources and social networks;
- school events that highlight performing arts, science fairs, community resources, and history days.

Table 8.1. Readiness of Teachers and Parents to Engage and Empower Students as Assessors

Acronym	Indicates/ Represents	Never	Rarely	Sometimes	Mostly
S	Student Standards Strategies	I really don't understand how to explain the standards and strategies to students and their parents.	It is difficult for students to explain the standards they are using for assignments and classwork.	Students can identify the expectations of an assignment if they are clearly described and demonstrated.	Students can explain what they are expected to do and ways to display their learning to others.
O	Ownership Organization Onus	Students are not engaged in their learning due to difficulties in understanding the purpose and process.	Students are marginally engaged in planning, learning, and self-assessing.	Students are engaged in their learning, and with guidance, can personalize their learning and outcomes.	Students are fully engaged in their learning and can personalize their own process and assessments.
A	Agency Accountability Achievement	Students do not feel responsible for their learning.	Students face some hurdles in holding themselves accountable for learning.	Students are generally accountable for their learning, depending on complexity and interest.	Students are able to explain their steps and outcomes and recommend adjustments to learning.
R	Results Review Respond	Students cannot reflect on their progress or ways to improve it.	With effort and support, students can reflect on their learning and identify areas for upgrading.	Students can typically reflect on their learning milestones and areas for improvement.	Students effectively reflect on and evaluate their learning and seek improvement.

1. Reflect on your overall readiness and make recommendations to support your own personal growth as well as developing students as engaged self-assessors and engaging parents in the process. Think about steps you can take and resources you can rely on.

2. Review your ratings and readiness to partner with parents. What steps can you take to strengthen their ability to engage with their children in their learning, progress, and outcomes?

Once parents become familiar with routines of students self-assessment, teachers can incorporate home-based self-assessment activities for students. Additionally, teachers can offer parents a self-rating scale so they can reflect on their skills and consider ways to strengthen them. Here are activities that support home-based assessments:

- Homework assignments that include a reflective and self-assessment exercise for parents and students to complete together
- Involving children in community and service projects in which they can monitor and celebrate successful outcomes
- Guiding parents to online resources for additional learning or for activities they can focus on with their children
- Collaboratively developing discussion points for family conversations about learning purposes, processes, and outcomes
- Bedtime check-ins that include reflections on shared readings or viewings or reciprocal questioning and journaling

PUTTING INTO PRACTICE

As teachers develop insights into their students' understanding of expected outcomes, the ability to see relevance in their learning, and an understanding of self-assessment, they are better prepared to help parents talk with their children about opportunities for learning and growth. Table 8.2 offers a checklist to reflect on current practices to fully engage parents in their students' self-assessments. Evaluate your current strategies for partnering with parents to support their children's learning through self-assessment activities at home and beyond the school day. Rate yourself on a 1 to 5 scale with 1 being never and 5 being always. Add actions for next steps you can or will take for added growth with each strategy.

TEACHERS CAN ENGAGE AND ENABLE PARENTS IN STUDENT SELF-ASSESSMENT

From the time a child is an infant, she continually self-assesses her development as she learns to raise her head and then turn her head from left to right when lying on her tummy. Several weeks later, she discovers that she can roll over. Months later she is creeping, then crawling, and eventually she is pulling up on furniture and taking her first steps. With a blink of the eye, she is running through the house. Throughout these physical, social, emotional, and cognitive developmental milestones, her parents are documenting progress with photos, recordings, and regular updates with the pediatrician.

Table 8.2. Checklist on Strategies That Support Partnering with Parents

Strategies for Partnering with Parents	Current Status	Desired Level	Proposed Actions for Added Growth
1. Regularly verify that students understand the learning intentions and content standards of their learning processes.			
2. Recognize and acknowledge students' individual learning challenges and successes.			
3. Differentiate students' learning needs by using effective classroom management and learning strategies.			
4. Routinely embed student self-assessments and reflections into daily learning.			
5. Encourage students to self-score and self-correct assessments and include necessary explanation and elaboration.			
6. Consider students' learning interests and offer choices and adaptable learning experiences to ensure engagement.			
7. Sequence student self-assessment strategies in ways that support developmental sequences, stages, and abilities.			
8. Provide students with opportunities to team-teach each other and collaborate for both supporting and extending learning.			
9. Share and elaborate on the SOAR Model with families throughout the school year through school activities, outreach, and notes.			
10. Include home-based self-assessment activities for students that guide students in assessing their homework as well as community engagement activities.			
11. Provide resources and information to parents on ways they can support their child's development in self-assessment.			

Throughout the preschool years, children explore the world around them and self-assess their many accomplishments and challenges. Most children are encouraged to explore at their own level of development. Others are limited due to their parents' control of the environment, safety concerns, or lack of resources. Some children may challenge the limits of their parents' control through creative and independent problem solving.

When students start school, they bring a wide range of experiences and abilities to the classroom. It is overwhelming for even the most experienced teachers to accommodate and understand the needs of a class of twenty-four or more students. Regardless of their students' prior learning experiences, classroom teachers have strategies and skills to accommodate for most of their students' variety of learning needs by relying on a range of instructional and school services.

As teachers get to know their students, they can meet with parents to understand how each student learns and experiences daily life at home. Some come from nurturing home environments. Others learn to be more self-sufficient as they return home each day to minimal resources or unsafe neighborhoods. It is important that teachers understand their students' backgrounds as well as rely on school leadership, psychologists, reading specialists, resource teachers, and others for additional guidance in support of students and families.

Teachers can also help parents recognize that their children can become self-assessors while completing their homework, home projects, and daily responsibilities. Self-assessment skills can be reinforced by parents when their children share their personalized learning portfolios that include student-created assessment tools and instruments. Teachers can design self-reflective questionnaires for students to complete at regular intervals. Learning can also be engaging, focused, and reflective at home and in the community. For example:

- Math calculation problems that include measuring a student's home for painting or carpeting, financial planning for vacations, budgeting for meal preparation, and building a container for a vegetable garden
- Science experiments that study watering vegetables under different conditions, electricity conservation strategies, water conservation options, and the impact of recycling programs in a community
- Computer coding and demonstrations of mastering digital productivity
- Social studies research on a student's ancestors or planning family trips to historical sites
- Providing and evaluating services that support the needs of community members, the homeless, seniors, and disabled

PARTNERING WITH PARENTS

Tables 8.3, 8.4, and 8.5 provide templates for teachers to reflect and plan ways they can support and partner with parents at home in reinforcing student-engaged assessments. Table 8.4 encourages parents to reflect on the evidence and observations of their child's self-assessment progress. It also incorporates a way to record their action plan, as well as ways they can help their child with their homework and other family and community activities that can support student-engaged assessments. The student reflective survey in table 8.5 can be used by students to identify how their parents were able to provide added learning support for homework completion and daily life activities.

Once teachers create an action plan for implementing these new instructional practices, they can create a parent and a student reflection worksheet that can be completed weekly. These forms can offer teachers added insight on how they can help students and their parents in developing extended learning opportunities outside of the classroom. In this way, students can start integrating their learning strategies into their daily lives and parents will gain insight on what their children are learning and how this learning impacts other activities in their lives.

As teachers receive these weekly reflections from parents, they can adjust the homework assignments to reinforce learning and recommend additional learning opportunities for children and their families. Table 8.5 is an example of a reflective self-assessment that students can use that corresponds to a parent's reflective assessment. These forms can be modified to support a specific grade level or individual teacher's needs.

Think about It

When teachers use similar reflective forms for parents and their children, families can share the results of these reflections. Students can teach their parents how they have used self-assessment as a vehicle that supports their learning. Parents can gain understanding about how their child is learning through various family and community activities. These insights can also help teachers create project-based learning activities that reinforce significant learning outcomes and are grade-level appropriate beyond the classroom. What are your thoughts about partnering with parents on student self-assessments?

Table 8.3. Teacher Reflection on Next Steps in Partnering with Parents to Engage Students in Self-Assessment

In the space below, outline your action plan to help parents become fully engaged in their children's self-assessment of activities in their homework as well as their daily lives.

Steps to Partner with Parents	My Personalized Action Plan
1. When will I discuss how students can self-assess their learning with parents (i.e., parent-teacher conferences, a parent workshop, or a classroom event)?	
2. How can I provide parents with an overview on grade-level standards relevant to homework and family activities?	
3. How will I demonstrate students' abilities to self-assess their learning through student portfolios, student self-assessed report cards, reflective grant development, or project-based learning reflective journals?	
4. How can students explain their learning in weekly homework assignments and daily household work (i.e., journaling, completing a questionnaire, or videotaping demonstrated competencies)?	
5. What skills or resources can my peers provide me to fully implement this student-learning strategy?	
6. Are there other areas of concern that I must address before implementing this instructional practice?	

Table 8.4. Parent Feedback and Reflection on Weekly Homework Assignments

In the space below, evaluate how your child was able to self-assess various homework assignments this week. Also, consider how your child has applied various learning applications to daily life responsibilities and family activities.

Child's Name: _____   Date: _____

Activity	Was my child able to apply self-assessment strategies to this activity? In what ways?	What self-assessment strategy did my child use (i.e., self-reporting of outcomes, structured reflection, etc.) in relation to attainment of goals?	What else did he/she observe or learn from this experience?
Homework Assignments: 1. 2. 3.	Yes............... No		
Type of weekly chore: 1. 2. 3.	Yes............... No		
Type of family activity: 1. 2. 3.	Yes............... No		
Type of community service activity: 1. 2. 3.	Yes............... No		
Other type of activity (i.e., vacation, game, family meeting, sporting event): 1. 2. 3.	Yes............... No		

Table 8.5. Student Reflection on How Parents Supported Their Learning on Weekly Homework Assignments

In the space below, evaluate how you were able to self-assess various homework assignments this week. Also, consider how you applied your learning to daily life, personal responsibilities, and family activities.

My Name: _____   Date: _____

Activity	Was I able to apply self-assessment strategies to this activity? In what ways?	What self-assessment strategy did I use (i.e., self-reporting of outcomes, structured reflection, etc.) in relation to attainment of goals?	What else did I observe or learn from this experience?
Homework assignments: 1. 2. 3.	Yes or No?		
Type of weekly chore: 1. 2. 3.	Yes or No?		
Type of family activity: 1. 2. 3.	Yes or No?		
Type of community service activity: 1. 2. 3.	Yes or No?		
Other type of activity (i.e., vacation, game, family meeting, sporting event): 1. 2. 3.	Yes or No?		

Chapter Nine

Conclusions and Next Steps

[*Testing has always been about hindsight.*]
It's good for seeing where you've been . . . but it can't tell you where you ought to go.

—Robert M. Pirsig

There is a long history of educational reform. From early Socratic dialogue to current large-scale testing, educators have persistently delved into students' understanding and earnestly tried to measure all types of learning outcomes. However, there are differences between testing and assessment. They both provide evidence of whether the goals of education are being met. Tests are more quantitative, while assessment includes more qualitative insights. Tests provide a snapshot of learning, while assessment delves more deeply into students' thinking and monitors progress toward mastery.

Tests are better suited for generating data about students' achievement during specified periods of time and are typically used to sort, rate, and rank, as well as compare schools and learners. They lead to monitoring and reporting of data on student, teacher, and school performance. Local assessments are generally less pervasive, offer deeper insights into student thinking, engage learners, and inform instructional decisions in the short term.

Equally important, if not more important than periodic tests, are ongoing and embedded assessments that engage learners and check progress in the here and now. Summarizing and practicing during learning are essential for developing student understanding before moving forward. These ongoing gauges reinforce and make learning linger as students continually reconsider what they have learned, what it means, how they can use it, and what may be next.

In one school, teachers decided it was important to begin new learning by having their students summarize their prior learning. Some teachers chose to rely on established teacher-led sessions, such as creating whole-class summary sheets. Other teachers turned over the responsibility for reviewing and summarizing to the students by having one group write quiz questions (this required fact checking) and another group answer the questions (this required consensus).

Keep in mind that reviews of standards-based learning intentions, such as putting things in the correct order (i.e., numbers, eras, or sequences), generally rely on more structured measures. Conceptual learning such as comparing, predicting, and designing may be better suited to flexible strategies that allow students to show their thinking along with drawing conclusions.

Think about it: There's an adage attributed to Benjamin Franklin, "Tell me and I forget; teach me and I remember; involve me and I learn." Adapting this for assessment, it might go like this: "Test me and I forget, involve me and I remember, hold me responsible and I become accountable." Think about how this is relevant in your setting. How can it be used by teachers in grade levels and content areas as well as applied schoolwide?

In the preface and throughout each chapter, the authors have introduced and explained the principles and guidelines for best practices in assessment. Review the diagram in figure 9.1 by identifying your priorities about what is most important in assessment. A brief list is provided, but feel free to use your own ideas and words to describe best practices. Discuss and compare your choices with others. In what ways are they similar and different? Why?

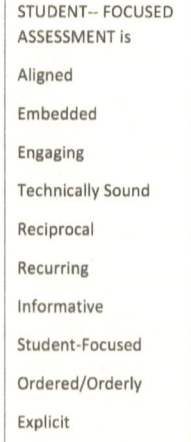

Figure 9.1.   Essentials of student-focused assessment

FUNDAMENTAL IDEALS

Sometimes educators are required to follow policy and procedures that are less than ideal for their students. Sometimes individuals and societies move forward, disregarding what has been learned through conflicts, triumphs, failures, and brilliant minds.

In his book, *Guns, Germs, and Steel*, Jared Diamond traces human history through the concept of "cargo," meaning the stuff that humans carry around with them. He explains that every culture has its cargo, whether it be material possessions, belief systems, or resources. There is much that still needs to be understood about assessment cargo and why it has been carried along for years. After all, standardized tests were first used during the Han Dynasty, thousands of years ago in China.

For educators, access to students' neurological networks would be ideal. For now, most teaching and learning decisions are based on the evidence of brain processing, often through test scores. But bigger numbers aren't necessarily better numbers: For example, consider the number of Facebook friends versus the number of close friends you can truly rely on when you have a problem.

Along with students' data, it's also important to consider their unique qualities, capacities, capabilities, and experiences. It is not easy to balance each student's educational abilities and needs with the expectations of rigorous educational testing. Meaningful learning outcomes are rarely described by numerical test scores. Rather, it is those aha moments when a student says, "I used to think ____. But now I realize ____." Or says, "Oh, now I see how that works!" or "Look, I got a better grade than on my first try."

Instead of persuasive marketing from educational vendors who promise higher achievement, maybe this is the time to engage learners with a version of JFK's words: "Ask what you can do to improve your own learning outcomes."

Most of the best advice about assessment is about balance: finding the hinge point between meeting the requirements of big data managers while informing minute-by-minute classroom practice. Take a moment to reconsider the questions raised throughout this book: What are your instructional purposes? How do you select assessments that support them? How can you engage learners in assessment and rely on the insights from formative processes to improve learning outcomes?

We live in transformative times, where breakthroughs in knowledge in manifold areas have become routine. It is also the best time to shape a balanced and reliable system of assessment. Three essential parts of this system are policy, preparation, and practice.

We are at a pivotal time in educational assessment when it is essential for all constituents to work together to balance all types of assessment and afford children multiple opportunities to show what they know and can do.

Figure 9.2. Next steps: finding balance

Policy

The Gordon Commission on the Future of Assessment in Education urges policy makers to move beyond large-scale assessments and recognize "that there are multiple types of assessment and that a better balance must be struck among them" (2013).

Joan Herman asserts, "I believe that by making our assessments more coherent in both design and use, we can create assessment systems which will measure the *right stuff* in the *right ways* while better serving intended purposes, particularly the purpose of improving teaching and learning" (2010, 1).

A reasoned policy based on input from multiple constituents that takes into consideration the needs of multiple users will best serve students, teachers, and schools today and in the future.

Preparation

On first look, formative assessment appears pretty straightforward: Gather evidence to find out what students know and decide how to respond to it. But a shift to accurate, embedded, engaging, and informative assessment requires a deeper understanding of the nitty-gritties and includes a toolbox of strategies to fit specific learning targets, as well as the ability to analyze and use the forthcoming data to inform responses.

Practice

Think for a moment about something you don't typically do well, such as playing basketball or a musical instrument, teaching an online class, or presenting before a large audience. You would most likely need some learning, rehearsal, guidance, and feedback as you develop your skills.

Whether it is included in preservice preparation or in-service coaching, the promise of using best practices in assessment can best be fulfilled when teachers understand the process for planning, engaging learners, analyzing data, and responding purposefully to assessments of learning. This culture, committed to best practice, is sustained through informed leadership, engaged students, and opportunities for continuous learning.

Think about It

There is adequate evidence that what happens in the classroom, the interactions between teachers and students, makes the biggest difference in learning outcomes. Whether you are a fan of visible learning (Hattie, 2012), differentiation (Tomlinson, 2014), understanding by design (Wiggins and McTighe, 2005), or other proven scaffolds and practices, the intention is to inform and guide local convention based on the belief that advancing student learning is dependent on putting assessment in teachers' and students' hands. Some ideas to consider:

- Maintain a respectful, growth-oriented classroom culture.
- Provide clear learning targets.
- Inform students of success criteria.
- Incorporate formative assessment throughout learning.
- Use questioning strategies to clarify and deepen learning.
- Engage students as co-assessors.
- Use feedback that is specific and actionable.
- Strategically adjust content, pacing, resources, and depth of learning.
- Rely on formative assessment to enable learning rather than quantify it.
- Seek ways to upskill what you are already doing well.

RETURNING ASSESSMENT TO EDUCATORS

There have been and continue to be more educational initiatives that would fill this page. Educators are being pulled in numerous and sometimes conflicting directions. As such, this seems like a good time to return educational assessment to the educators rather than using it as a channel for enforcing state and federal policy and funding. Of course, accountability is needed, but without finger-pointing and high-stakes repercussions. Instead, offer clear expectations, fair quotas, and consistent processes for accountability. When students, as well as teachers, feel respected, included, and expectant, they are more willing to try new things and accept that success comes from step-by-step progress.

Educators require support and guidance about how to transfer responsibility for learning outcomes to students. A novice figure skater would never fall down on the ice, point her finger, or blame his coach. Kristi Yamaguchi and Brian Boitano would have pulled themselves up, brushed off the ice flakes, analyzed what happened, ask their coach for advice, and try another axel.

As the scores on NAEP (the USDE's National Assessment of Educational Progress) and other large-scale measures have become stagnant, it is essential to ask if we are teaching and assessing the right things in the right way. There's a place for large-scale measures just as there is a place for classroom assessments.

As education has become more commercialized, it is more important than ever to return to the fundamental best practices of assessment. Steer clear of the persistent voices, impossible claims, and promises of success for all. Success is different for each student. Not everyone will become an influencer or game designer. Some will be counselors, teachers, and chefs; others specialists in acupuncture, anthropology, and coral reefs, and still others forecasters and developers of new forms of energy or human transport.

DEVELOPING ACCOUNTABLE LEARNERS

In addition to asking teachers to adjust classroom assessment practices, it makes sense to also involve learners in thinking about their processes and progress. The educators whose stories are told in this book helped students believe that they could reflect on their learning, cultivate self-regulation, and make purposeful modifications to learning. But, no one is an expert from the beginning, so pick your own starting point, rehearse and practice your ideas with supportive colleagues, and keep an open mind when trying new things. In doing so, students will come to understand that it is okay to venture into new territory (with a pal if needed) and embrace opportunities for learning. In this way, students will feel accountable without the fear of long-term consequences for less-than-stellar outcomes on their first try.

NEXT STEPS: CUSTOMIZE AND PERSONALIZE FOR YOUR OWN SETTING

Start by considering your local community and schools and what will best meet their needs. Here are three steps to begin your quest.

Step 1. Determine where your system and teachers currently are in each step of the student engagement and empowerment process. Are students assessment ready?

- How can we prepare all students to be assessment ready?
- What are the best ways to engage students in assessment?
- How can we support students as owners and monitors of their own assessment?
- What does it take to develop them as agents and managers of assessment?

Step 2. Start your plan based on the conditions in your current assessment practices. This may require bolstering a whole school foundation on the basics of self-assessment while also personalizing the process for individual learners who may need additional support or opportunities to soar higher.

Step 3. Revisit the fundamental principles and elements of best practice in effective assessment: Identify areas of strength and also aspects of practice that you would like to strengthen. Be sure to keep the focus on students and learning. Here's a brief review:

- *Assessment is mutual and monitored:* It is systemically aligned, supportive, engaging, as well as sequenced and reciprocal with learning purposes and learners.
- *Assessment is useful and informative:* Students and teachers understand the goals and their sequence, the underlying principles and learning intentions, as well as the meaning and significance of assessment outcomes.
- *Assessment is sticky:* It is a part of learning that raises attention and increases interest, as it is responsive to students' abilities and outcomes. It is focused, embedded, and recurrent throughout teaching and learning.
- *Assessment is technically sound:* It is valid, meaning it measures the intended targets, and reliable, meaning consistent and congruent with learning and free from bias.

Validate: Rely on Established and Verified Research and Practice

Avoid the hype, propaganda, misinformation, deception, and half-truths that may accompany powerful marketing. Celebrities are often people who are known for being well-known. The National Institutes of Health have prepared an explanation of how to use research in education (Stanovich and Stanovich, 2013).

Just because someone has a lot of followers doesn't mean that person is an authority. Rather, we need to seek influential experts in educational assessment. Those who share substantiated ideas and nonbiased resources include Linda-Darling Hammond, Thomas Guskey, Dylan Wiliam, Margaret Heritage, Larry Ferlazzo, Heidi Andrade, Michael Fullan, John Hattie, and James McMillan, as well as noted research universities, including UCLA Center for Educational Assessment, Vanderbilt University, UConn Neag School of Education, Columbia University, University of Pennsylvania, Stanford, and Johns Hopkins.

Depend on Reliable Brain Science

Throughout the book, you've heard about the importance of understanding the brain and how emotions take control during stressful situations. For most of us, tests are stressful, and while there is a place for infrequent large-scale, high-stakes, and selected-choice measures of learning, they are not the best assessments for the classroom. In classrooms, routine embedded assessments are meant to serve students and are a foundation for learning when they are based on divergent rather than convergent responses, encourage reflection and analysis, and increase intrinsic motivation for learning. Read more on Glenn Whitman and Mariale Hardiman's research (2014), which explains the role of brain science in educational assessment.

Rely on and Respect What Is Substantiated and Sustainable

While innovation has generally served education well, frequent shifts in resources and ever-changing learning targets disrupt and interrupt learning rather than facilitate it. It is more useful to depend on practices that have been confirmed and substantiated over time than on unproven distractions. Consider the following ways that you can use the research-based ideas in this book for preparing and engaging learners as well as developing them as owners and agents of assessment. How can you apply and utilize each of these essential actions for empowering students as assessors?

1. A sense of well-being is an essential foundation for feeling safe when being assessed and measured.
2. Understanding expectations and learning intentions helps students formulate plans and strategies for their learning.
3. Deconstructing learning goals and processes become actionable for students.
4. Assessments that align with learning intentions are most worthwhile and effective.
5. Assessments embedded throughout learning bring to light lingering misconceptions.
6. Progress and stumbling blocks become visible through routine assessments.
7. When students become self-assessors, they have opportunities to personalize and optimize learning.
8. Routine feedback and follow-up that is specific, actionable, and forward-thinking, is essential to progress.
9. Personal reflection, as well as informative feedback from peers and teachers, is worthwhile.
10. As students develop agency, they begin to manage and regulate their own learning and assessment and in turn become more accountable.
11. Multiple assessment methods and choice in showing learning build confidence and engage students.

Do

Keep in mind that everyone has biases and blind spots from their unique life experiences. Alternatively, when you hear an idea repeated by a known and respected source, you are subject to confirmation bias. At the end of the day, teachers are all human, doing the best they can with what is known about assessment and unraveling new ideas. Be gentle with each other because if you do so, students will SOAR and develop essential life skills by

- developing self-monitoring and self-regulation;
- understanding the value and benefits of taking personal responsibility and working with and learning from others;
- transferring skills of effective engagement ownership and agency to other aspects of life;
- incorporating low-stress and low-stakes assessments.

In schools, assessment is best kept in the hands of assessment experts, including the teachers who know and understand their students, have deep

130   *Chapter Nine*

knowledge of their subject, and utilize the best practices in instructional assessment. Still, there are many teachers who need support and guidance. This is true for both new teachers who may have taken one course in educational assessment during their studies and for veteran teachers who may need help adapting/modifying their traditional practices to align with and support the nitty-gritties of education today.

Think of assessment as the invisible gorilla on the stage (see https://www.youtube.com/watch?v=IGQmdoK_ZfY). While you are busy focusing on tests, testing, and test scores, it's easy to lose track of the invisible gorilla or miss the camel poking his nose into the tent. If you don't, the gorilla will take center stage and soon the whole camel will be in the tent.

Figure 9.3.   Don't let the camel's nose into the tent

Keep these ideas about assessment at the forefront:

- Assessment is a strategy for furthering learning.
- Comprehensive assessment requires the use of varied types of assessment for multiple purposes.
- Assessment of learning in the form of final scores should hold no surprises for teachers or students.
- Engaging students in assessment and *as* assessors is imperative.
- Utilize multipurpose, multiuse learning and assessments.

- Refocus assessment as a *form of learning* rather than solely as a measure of final outcomes. Assessment is not the final step. It requires a response: "What do we do now?"
- Seek multiple viewpoints on assessment, from the firmament to the microscopic level.

This book began with a discussion of purposeful assessment. It weaves theory and research into real-world opportunities for learning and assessing. Start your process by taking a step in that direction. Select your purpose, choose your strategies, build your skills, and collaborate with others. Everyone plays a role in improving educational practices and policies. Whatever your role is, make sure your voice is heard. Valuable work is worth doing well.

> Coming together is a beginning, keeping together is progress, working together is success.
>
> —Henry Ford

Bibliography

Andrade, H., Huff, K., & Brooke, G. (2012). *Assessing learning.* Students at the Center Series. Retrieved from https://studentsatthecenterhub.org/wp-content/uploads/2015/10/Assessing-Learning-Students-at-the-Center-1.pdf.

Bae, S., & Kokka, K. (2016). *Student engagement in assessments: What students and teachers find engaging.* Stanford, CA: Stanford Center for Opportunity Policy in Education. Retrieved from https://edpolicy.stanford.edu/sites/default/files/publications/student-engagement-assessments-final.pdf.

Black, P., & Wiliam, D. (2010). Inside the black box: Raising standards through classroom assessment. *Phi Beta Kappan, 92*(1), 81–90.

Brookhart, S., Moss, C., & Long, B. (2008, November). Formative assessment that empowers. *Educational Leadership, 66*(3): 52–57. Retrieved from http://www.ascd.org/publications/educational-leadership/nov08/vol66/num03/Formative-Assessment-That-Empowers.aspx.

Burke, M. (2018, April 6). Empower your students to design and fund their own project-based learning experiences. *Corwin Connect* [Blog]. Retrieved from https://corwin-connect.com/2018/04/empower-your-students-to-design-and-fund-their-own-project-based-learning-experiences/.

California Department of Education. (2013). *California common core state standards: English language arts and literacy in history/social studies, science, and technical subjects.* Sacramento, CA: California Department of Education.

Common Core State Standards (2016). *Supplemental information for Appendix A of the Common Core State Standards for English Language Arts and Literacy: New research on text complexity.* Retrieved from http://www.corestandards.org/assets/E0813_Appendix_A_New_Research_on_Text_Complexity.pdf.

Conley, D. T., & Darling-Hammond, L. (2013). *Creating systems of assessment for deeper learning.* Stanford, CA: Stanford Center for Opportunity in Education. Retrieved from https://edpolicy.stanford.edu/sites/default/files/publications/creating-systems-assessment-deeper-learning_0.pdf.

Csikszentmihalyi, M. (2008). *Flow: The psychology of optimal experience.* New York: Harper Perennial Modern Classics.

Dewey, J. (1910). *How we think.* Lexington, MA: D.C. Heath and Company.

Dyer, K. (2014, March 20). Proof that student self-assessment moves learning forward. NWEA measuring what matters. NWEA, *Teach Learn Grow* [Blog.]. Retrieved from https://www.nwea.org/blog/2014/proof-student-self-assessment-moves-learning-forward/.

Dyer, K. (2015, September 17). Research proof points—better student engagement improves student learning. NWEA, *Teach Learn Grow* [Blog]. Retrieved from https://www.nwea.org/blog/2015/research-proof-points-better-student-engagement-improves-student-learning/.

Eisner, E. (1999, May). The uses and limits of performance assessments. *Phi Delta Kappan, 80*(9) 658–60.

Ferguson, R. F., Phillips, S. F., Rowles, J. F. S., & Friendlander, J. W. (2015). *The influence of teaching: Beyond standardized test scores: Engagement, mindset, and agency.* Seattle, WA: Raikes Foundation.

Ferlazzo, L. (2014). The secret sauce of formative assessment. *EdWeek Teacher.* Retrieved from http://blogs.edweek.org/teachers/classroom_qa_with_larry_ferlazzo/2014/12/response_the_secret_sauce_of_formative_assessment.html.

Ferlazzo, L. (2017, March 7). Response: Bloom's and SOLO are not just colorful posters we hang on the wall. *EdWeek Teacher.* Retrieved from http://blogs.edweek.org/teachers/classroom_qa_with_larry_ferlazzo/2017/03/response_blooms_solo_are_not_just_colorful_posters_we_hang_on_the_wall.html.

Fredricks, J. A., & McCloskey, W. (2012). The measurement of student engagement: A comparative analysis of various methods and student self-report instruments. In S. L. Christenson et al. (Eds.), *Handbook of research on student engagement* (p. 763). New York: Springer Science and Business Media.

Frey, N., Fisher, D., & Hattie, J. (2018, February). Developing "assessment capable" learners. *Educational Leadership, 75*(5): 46–51.

Gordon Commission on the Future of Assessment in Education. (2013). "A public policy statement." Retrieved from https://www.ets.org/Media/Research/pdf/gordon_commission_public_policy_report.pdf.

Greene, J. P., and McShane, M. Q. (2018, April 30). Learning from failure. *Phi Delta Kappan.* Retrieved from https://www.kappanonline.org/greene-mcshane-school-reforms-failure-learning-education-leaders/.

Hattie, J. (2012). *Visible learning for teachers: Maximizing impact on learning.* New York: Routledge.

Herman, J. L. (2010). *Coherence: Key to next generation assessment success* (AACC Report). Los Angeles, CA: University of California. Retrieved from https://files.eric.ed.gov/fulltext/ED524221.pdf.

Hough, L (2015, Summer). Does it have to be so complicated? *Harvard Education Magazine,* Harvard Graduate School of Education.

Klinger, D. A., McDivitt, P. R., Howard, B. B., Munoz, M. A., Rogers, W. T., & Wylie, E. C. (2015). *The classroom assessment standards for PreK–12 teachers.*

Kindle Direct Press. Retrieved from http://www.jcsee.org/the-classroom-assessment-standards-new-standards.

Kruger, J., & Dunning, D. (1999). Unskilled and unaware of it: How difficulties in recognizing one's own incompetence lead to inflated self-assessments. *Journal of Personality and Social Psychology, 77*, 1121–1134.

La Marca, P. M., Redfield, D., & Winter, P. C. (2000). *State standards and state assessment systems: A guide to alignment.* Washington, DC: Council of Chief State School Officers. Retrieved from https://www.gpo.gov/fdsys/pkg/ERIC-ED466497/pdf/ERIC-ED466497.pdf.

Lynch, M. (2018, April 26). What happens when students own their learning? *The Edvocate.* Retrieved from https://www.theedadvocate.org/what-happens-when-students-own-their-learning/.

Maslow A. H. (1943). A theory of human motivation. *Psychological Review, 50*(4), 370–396.

McCormick, M., Cappella, E., & O'Connor E. (2015). Social-emotional learning and academic achievement: Using causal methods to explore classroom-level mechanisms. *Aera Open, 1*(3). Retrieved from https://journals.sagepub.com/doi/full/10.1177/2332858415603959.

McMillan, J. H., & Hearn, H. (2008, Fall). Student self-assessment: The key to stronger student motivation. *Educational Horizons,* 40–49. Retrieved from https://files.eric.ed.gov/fulltext/EJ815370.pdf.

Palomba, C., & Banta, T. (1999.) *Assessment essentials.* San Francisco, CA: Jossey-Bass.

Panadero, E., Jonsson A., & Botella, J. (2017). Effects of self-assessment on self-regulated learning and self-efficacy: Four meta-analyses. *Education Research Review, 22*, 74–98.

Perie, M., Marion, S., Gong, B., & Wurtzel, J. (2007). *The role of interim assessment in a comprehensive assessment system: A partnership of achievement.* Washington, DC: The Aspen Institute and Center for Assessment.

Ross, J. A. (2006). The reliability, validity, and utility of self-assessment. *Practical Assessment Research and Evaluation, 11*(10). Retrieved from https://pareonline.net/pdf/v11n10.pdf.

Rugen, L., Woodfin, L., & Berger, R. (2014). *Leaders of their own learning: Transforming schools through student-engaged assessment.* San Francisco: Jossey-Bass.

Sadler, D. R. (1998). Formative assessment: Revisiting the territory. *Assessment in Education: Principles, Policy and Practice, 1*(5), 77–84.

Shearer, E., & Gottfried, J. (2017, September 7). News use across social media platforms. *Pew Research Center.* Retrieved from http://www.journalism.org/2017/09/07/news-use-across-social-media-platforms-2017/.

Shepard, L. A. (2000). The role of assessment in a learning culture. *Educational Researcher, 27*(7) 4–14. Retrieved from http://math.arizona.edu/~cemela/english/content/shortcourses/assessment/Day%202%20Reading%202.pdf.

Spencer, John. (2017, December 3). Five ways to boost student engagement with flow theory. *John Spencer* [Blog]. Retrieved from http://www.spencerauthor.com/flow-theory/.

Stanovich, P. J., & Stanovich, K. E. (2013). *Using research and reason in education: How teachers can use scientifically based research to make curricular and instructional decisions*. National Institute for Literacy. Retrieved from https://www.nichd.nih.gov/publications/pubs/using_research_stanovich.

Stenger, M. (2014, August 6) 5 Research-based tips for providing students with meaningful feedback. *Edutopia*. Retrieved from https://www.edutopia.org/blog/tips-providing-students-meaningful-feedback-marianne-stenger.

Strauss, V. (2013, September 27). "Bill Gates: "It would be great if our education stuff worked but . . ." *Washington Post*. Retrieved from https://www.washingtonpost.com/news/answer-sheet/wp/2013/09/27/bill-gates-it-would-be-great-if-our-education-stuff-worked-but/?noredirect=on&utm_term=.702436e8a5de.

Taylor, L., & Parsons, J. (2011). Improving student engagement. *Current Issues in Education, 14*(1). http://cie.asu.edu/.

Tomlinson, C. A. (2014). *The differentiated classroom: Responding to the needs of all learners*. 2nd revised edition. Alexandria, VA: Association for Supervision and Curriculum Development.

Tough, Paul. (2013). *How children succeed*. New York: Houghton Mifflin.

Tyler, R. W., Gagne, R. M., & Scriven, M. (Eds.). (1967). *Perspectives of curriculum evaluation*. American Educational Research Association Monograph Series on Curriculum Evaluation. Chicago: Rand McNally.

Whitman, G., & Hardiman, M. (2014, Winter) *Assessment and the learning brain*. National Association of Independent Schools. Retrieved from https://www.nais.org/magazine/independent-school/winter-2014/assessment-and-the-learning-brain/.

Wiggins, G., & McTighe, J. (2005). *Understanding by design*. 2nd expanded edition. Alexandria, VA: Association for Supervision and Curriculum Development.

Wiliam, D. (2011). *Embedded formative assessment*. Bloomington, IN: Solution Tree.

Wiliam, D. (2018, March 20). *The difference between assessment and testing*. Learning Sciences International. Retrieved from https://blog.learningsciences.com/2018/03/20/the-difference-between-assessment-and-testing/.

Index

accountability, 15, 22, 44, 72, 73, 79, 98, 101, 102, 127
achievement, 15, 34, 35, 41, 59; evidence of, 29, 56, 79, 89, 95, 105
agency: advantages for students, 85; students as agents of assessment, 15, 21, 23, 79, 82–85
align, 20, 26, 28, 46, 50, 55, 60, 73, 86, 92, 105, 129
annotate, 5, 45, 89, 94
apply, 9, 10, 13, 54, 67, 76, 91, 92, 120, 128
appropriate challenge, 86
assessment: ready, 22, 29, 36–38, 40–48; learners, 33–37; schools, 37–38; systems, 124; that engage, 62–65. *See also* engagement; evidence
assessment-capable learners, 69, 70, 71, 77, 79, 87. *See also* ownership
assidere, 54
attention/attention span, 35, 61, 62, 127

balance and balanced assessment, 18, 28, 48, 52, 86, 123, 124
best practice in assessment, xix, xx, 25, 26
big picture, 6, 15, 19, 33, 38, 44, 59, 75
brain-friendly assessment, 37, 84, 128

challenge, 54; in assessment, 86
choice, 77, 90, 91; board, 92
clarity, 85–87
climate, classroom and school, 37
Common Core Standards, 6, 26. *See also* standards
control, 70
culture, classroom and school, 37
curiosity, 34, 42, 62

deconstruct standards, 4, 18, 23, 29, 37, 38, 39, 54, 86, 90
designing assessment, xix, 40, 44
diagnostic assessment, 75
differentiate, 27, 51
disengagement, 59
display learning, 18, 20, 29, 49, 51, 71, 72, 77
distractions, 26, 35, 63, 72

effective assessment, 6, 18, 25, 26, 27, 37, 65, 66
empowering students as assessors, 73, 75, 87, 90–94, 105
engage, 17, 66
engagement, 11, 23, 35, 49–67, 73, 81, 93; as motivation, 51–52; checklist, 60; into ownership, 72–73; and

137

SMART goals, 55; strategies, 53–56; that engage, 63–64
engaging reluctant learners, 59–60
evidence 28, 52, 59, 60, 65, 80, 105, 123

family partnerships, 111, 112, 114
feedback 5, 7, 45, 54, 60, 62, 66, 75, 79, 84, 86, 89, 102, 118, 129
focus, 27, 28, 53, 63–64, 66
formative assessment, 8, 21–22, 29, 45, 61, 65, 76
foundations: of readiness, xx, 28; of success, 3–6, 22, 26–29, 36

gaps, 23, 93
goals, goal setting, 23, 71, 100, 101
growth, 8, 18, 36; mindset, 52, 71

higher and deeper thinking and learning, 16, 71

improvement focus, 35
individualized, 18
informative, 5, 19, 65
interpersonal skills, 35

knowledge, xx, 8, 10, 13, 35, 40, 55, 76, 94–95, 101

learning intentions, personalize, 5
learning purpose, intentions and targets, xx, 4, 15, 74, 77
lenses of assessment, 34, 71
lesson plan and design, 28

Maslow's hierarchy, 4, 5
meaning, 6, 10, 16, 53, 62, 64, 86
measurable, 6–8, 23, 24, 46, 75, 84, 121, 126
mindsets, 36, 72, 101
mistakes as learning, 75
monitoring learning, 74, 76, 78
motivation, 17, 51–53, 73, 93, 98–100

non-cognitive, 72–74, 86, 88
non-negotiables of assessment, 26–27

opportunity, 76
outcomes, criteria and measures of, 92–95, 123, 131
ownership, 15, 19, 21–24, 45; of assessment, 59, 67, 69–70; benefits, 70–72; benefits for students, 71–81, 94; results, 67; by students, 74, 75. *See also* assessment capable learners; engagement, into ownership

parents as partners, 114, 117. *See* family partnerships
personal responsibility, 35
personalize, xix, xx, 20, 56–57, 94, 95
planning, 66, 71, 73–75, 77
policy, 124
preparing students for assessment, 37, 124
proactive assessment, 7–8
problem solving, 20, 71
progress, 16, 72

quality assessment, 85–87

rating scales, 98, 99
readiness for assessment, 33–38, 45–47
reciprocal, 75
reflections, 112, 117, 118, 119
relevance in assessment, 18, 51, 55, 86, 88, 95
responsive, 65
results, 15, 23
revision, 87–88, 96
rote learning, 63
routines, 49, 60, 75
rubrics and rating scales, 40, 41, 42, 46, 80, 97, 100, 101

scaffolds, 66
self-advocacy, 72
self-assessment, 92–96, 101

self-awareness, 45
self-monitor, 97, 120
self-regulation, 11, 71–72, 75, 78
sequences/steps in learning/assessing, 15, 16, 21, 23, 27, 36, 44, 61, 73, 74, 80, 96, 114, 115, 127
SMART goals, 55–56, 59
SOAR Model, 14, 15, 23, 44, 55, 59, 79, 89, 105
social-emotional skills, 74
standards, 16. *See also* deconstruct standards
steps and sequences in learning and assessing, 15, 16, 21, 23, 27, 36, 44, 61, 73, 74, 80, 96, 114, 115, 127
stress, 37, 38, 54

student: agency, 83–85; focused assessment, 8–9
student lens on assessment, 85
students: as designers of assessment, 87–88; at the center, 7, 8
success criteria, 40, 75, 77
support, 23, 66

tests vs. assessment, 9–10
thinking skills, 71
tracking/monitoring progress, 76, 93
transfer of ownership and responsibility, 43–45

valid and reliable assessment, 127–128
voice and choice, 45, 56, 77, 81, 86–87, 90–95

About the Authors

Laura Greenstein has been an educator for more than thirty years, serving as a teacher, department chair, and school leader in multiple grades and subjects. Dr. Greenstein combines this background with her experience as a school board member and professional development specialist to bring fresh and original ideas to educators about teaching, learning, and assessing. She consults with schools and districts and presents at workshops and conferences locally and nationally. As an adjunct professor at the University of Connecticut and the University of New Haven, she taught assessment as well as human development to undergraduate and graduate students.

Her work has been published in ASCD's *Educational Leadership*, *Corwin Connect*, *EdWeek*, *NASSP Bulletin*, and *Phi Delta Kappan*. Published books include: *What Teachers Really Need to Know about Formative Assessment* (2010), *Assessing 21st Century Skills* (2014), *Sticky Assessment: Classroom Strategies to Amplify Student Learning* (2016), and *Restorative Assessment: Strength-Based Practices That Support All Learners* (2018).

Laura dedicates this book to her inspirational family: Sloane, Riley, Andrew, Casey, and Catherine, who continuously support and encourage her. Their guidance and role modeling, each in their own extraordinary way, sustains her.

Mary Ann Burke is the cofounder of the *GenParenting* blog at www.genparenting.com and has written regularly for the *Corwin Connect* blog. Her research and publications focus on student-centered achievement. She has served as a credentialed parent educator and adjunct professor for over thirty years in California's schools. Dr. Burke has presented effective parenting and school engagement strategies at numerous state and national parent engagement events. Mary Ann previously led the Santa Clara County Office of

Education's Parent Engagement Initiative that serves as a state model for best practices in parent engagement for culturally diverse families. She is an active grandmother of five grandchildren and is the coauthor of *Effective Parenting! Capable Kids!* (2017).

Mary Ann has published books, articles, and blog posts on student achievement, effective parenting, community engagement in schools, and grant writing. Her books include *Developing Community-Empowered Schools* (2001), *Simplified Grantwriting* (2002), *Leveraging Resources for Student Success* (2002), and edited *Improving Achievement in Low-Performing Schools* (2004). She shares her expertise with educators and school leaders as a trainer, author, curriculum developer, and elementary school substitute teacher.

Mary Ann dedicates this book to her grandchildren who continue to inspire her with their learning antics and discoveries. They keep her young at heart and ready to learn.

www.ingramcontent.com/pod-product-compliance
Lightning Source LLC
Chambersburg PA
CBHW030140240426
43672CB00005B/203